# Fistful o' Zombies

EDEN STUDIOS PRESENTS A SHY/VASILAKOS PRODUCTION

# Fistful o' Zombies™

Produced by M. ALEXANDER JURKAT GEORGE VASILAKOS

Directed by GEORGE VASILAKOS

Written by SHANE LACY HENSLEY Additional Material by DANIEL HOLMES
THOM MARRION TOM REDDING GERRY SARACCO
DEREK STOELTING RAFAEL VELEZ

Editing by M. ALEXANDER JURKAT

Proofing by JEREMY HUNT, JACK KESSLER, KATIE KLOCEK

Director of Photography GEORGE VASILAKOS

Cover by GEORGE VASILAKOS

Visual Effects by THOMAS DENMARK TALON COLE DUNNING
JON HODGSEN CHRIS KEEFE GINGER KUBIC
LOSTON WALLACE MATT MORROW

Playtesting by ANDREW CIOTTI RUSH DUNCAN NICOL DUNCAN
DAVID FISHMAN THOMAS MACALUSO DANNY RIVERA
GERRY SARACCO

Based on the Original Concept by
CHRISTOPHER SHY and GEORGE VASILAKOS

# WWW.ALLFLESH.COM

**Eden Studios**
**6 Dogwood Lane, Loudonville, NY 12211**

Comments and questions can be directed via the Internet at www.allflesh.com, via e-mail at edenprod@aol.com or via letter with a self-addressed stamped envelope.

First Printing, February 2003
Stock EDN8003    ISBN 1-891153-84-6
Printed in Canada

# TABLE OF CONTENTS

Chapter One: Go West . . . . . . . . . . . . . . . 4

Chapter Two: The Good, the Bad, and the Dead . . . 16

Chapter Three: Singing Cowboys . . . . . . . . . . 44

Chapter Four: True Grit . . . . . . . . . . . . . 64

Chapter Five: Spaghetti with Meat . . . . . . . . 82

Chapter Six: Dances with Zombies . . . . . . . . . 98

Chapter Seven: Other Settings . . . . . . . . . . 116

Deadlands Conversion Notes . . . . . . . . . . . . 136

Index . . . . . . . . . . . . . . . . . . . . . . 142

# CHAPTER ONE

# GO WEST

**The** sun was hard on Texas. It didn't so much shine on the Lone Star State as glare at it angrily. Biting flies and scorpions were in league with the hateful thing, doing their best to keep people and beasts indoors. In the darkness.

That's where Flint sat on a hot summer day—in a dark, dirty cantina somewhere just south of the Texas border. His low, flat hat shadowed steely blue eyes and a roughly-shaven square jaw. His serape hid his hands. And his guns.

Like the weather, the tequila was warm. Even the worm at the bottom of the bottle had likely given in to the heat.

Hector Ramirez entered the cantina. Like everyone else who wasn't in siesta, sweat dripped off him in torrents. Flint's nose twitched at the smell. Hector smelled like a pig.

Hector ordered a drink—the same stomach-eating tequila Flint had been nursing all afternoon. Flint was about to stand when the other two members of Hector's gang stepped through the swinging doors. One of them glanced at Flint, dismissed him, then shared Hector's bottle. The three amigos glared at the bartender until he moved to the other end of the bar, and started discussing something in conspiratorial tones.

Flint studied his prey carefully. He watched how they drank, how their sure fingers clasped the perspiring shot glasses or the bottle. He saw how they all turned in unison when someone new entered the bar, or at the creak of leather that might indicate a gun sliding from a holster. They were fat, greasy, and stupid, but they were all veteran killers. Hector was wanted alive. Some bank in Texas wanted the money he'd stolen back, and Hector was reportedly the only one who knew where it was. That would be tough. The other two, however, were wanted dead or alive. That made them meat.

Flint had a plan. But his plans had a way of going to Hell.

One of the three, Julio, grabbed the bottle and moved to Flint's table. "Get up, gringo. Thees ees our table."

Flint's hand moved under his serape. Julio drew fast, the other two a second slower. Flint would remember that. From under the table, he slowly brought out a small knife. Julio wiped sweat from his mouth with his arm and cocked the gun pointing at the stranger. "Chu gonna pull a knife on me, gringo? Can't you see my pistola?" Julio laughed, and looked back at Hector and the other man, Jauquin, for approval. Flint would remember that too.

The gunslinger slowly scratched something on the table.

Julio watched in amazement. "Are you loco, gringo? I said geet up! Thees ees our table!"

Flint kept scratching. Slowly. Deliberately.

Julio moved slightly to Flint's right, trying to see the words the strange American scratched on the table.

"Kill heem!" said Hector. "Stoopeed yanqui dog!"

Julio fired off a shot. It splintered the wood behind Flint's head and silenced the rest of the cantina. The bartender's hand slid quietly under the bar, but Hector raised and cocked his single-action revolver in one smooth motion. "I wouldn't, amigo," he warned the man.

Flint jammed the knife into the table and slowly raised his head, letting Julio see his twitching blue eyes for the first time. The Mexican backed up a step. There was something in the gringo's stare that made his piss want to run out of his groin. But he was no wet-nosed kid who soiled himself in a gunfight. He'd killed four men and a score of Indians. Hector and Jauquin were right behind him. Losing face in front of them was almost as bad as a bullet in the gut.

"Stoopeed gringo!" he yelled again, spitting straight in Flint's face. "Ablo Englais? I said thees ees our table!"

The gunslinger's eyes twitched one last time. Then he pointed to what he'd carved on the dirty table.

Julio leaned in cautiously. "Julio Murietta, Hector Ram—eh?"

"It is your table, amigo," Flint growled. "Your names are right there."

Hector realized what it meant first—he was definitely the brains of the outfit. "He knows who we are, Julio."

Flint smiled and put one finger on the knife stuck in the table. He pulled it back almost to the point of breaking then let it go. The heavy blade snapped toward Julio and stabbed him in the thigh. Before he could scream, Flint drew down. He fanned three shots into Julio, put three more into Jauquin, then used the stunned Julio as a shield from the hasty bullets that erupted from Hector's gun. Julio slumped in his arms, dead weight. Jauquin danced like a fresh-killed chicken, twitching and firing random shots in his death spiral.

Hector stared in shock. His amigos had died in less than a heartbeat. But the gringo had fired six times. "You are empty, amigo!" he grunted, smiling nervously.

Something poked out from under Flint's serape. "This don't mean I'm happy to see you, Hector. I'm the two-gun type."

Hector looked nervously at the shape beneath the serape. "You're bluffing."

Julio groaned at Flint's feet. Not quite dead. His bloody hands stretched out for his pistol lying on the floor. Flint stepped on the bandit's hand without looking. Something popped and then cracked beneath his boots.

Flint leaned down, never taking his eyes off Hector, and took a fresh cigar and a long match from Julio. He drew the match along the bandit's skull and it hissed to life. The gunslinger stood, jammed the cigar in his teeth, then lit it. "Maybe," he said through his teeth.

Hector laughed. "Ha ha, gringo! You have cajones! But you do not have a second gun!"

A shot thundered in the small cantina. Hector looked down to see a small hole in the thick, meaty part of his leg. Blood spilled from the hole, thick and red. The bandit watched in shock as it ran down into his boot, then dribbled out onto the dirty floor before dripping down the cracks to the dirt below.

Hector dropped his gun.

\* \* \*

"Maybe we could split my compadres' bounty, gringo."

"Why would I wanna do that, Hector," the gunslinger rasped. He had bound Hector with rope to a dead tree. He leaned against his saddle, trying his best to cool down. The hateful sun had gone down hours ago. Now the Texas prairie was dark, and the night wind blew a cool breeze over the day's sweat. It was another two days to El Paso, where Flint could collect his reward. One thousand dollars for Hector, two hundred fifty a piece for the two rotting cadavers he'd thrown over the bandits' confiscated horses. Flint would sell those, too.

"You take these two in and collect the moola. I'll wait outside town for you to come back, then we split. Sixty-forty."

Flint stared at Hector incredulously. "You do realize you're tied to a log in the middle of Texas, don't you amigo?"

Hector smiled. "Ci. But do you know what I'm wanted for?"

Flint nodded. "Rustlin', thievin', murder."

"Not by the Americanos. By the Mexicans."

Flint shook his head. He knew the gang was wanted on both sides of the border, but dollars were worth more than pesos, so he hadn't bothered to learn about Ramirez's crimes in Mexico.

"They say I am 'El Diablo!'" Ramirez cackled. "The people say I am a sorcerer. That I can raise the dead."

Flint went back to his cigar. Hector was loco as a starving mule in a peyote field.

Hector closed his eyes and stared at the night sky. "*Ixcaret yecth atatl.*"

Flint ignored the bandit. He slumped down against his saddle and pulled his hat low to catch some shut-eye. "Gonna be a long day tomorrow, Hector. Ridin' in the sun out here's hard enough. 'Specially when you're draped over a saddle. I'd get some sleep if I were you."

Hector merely repeated the strange words. Flint spared the thief one last glance to make sure he was securely bound, then rolled over and went to sleep.

Strange dreams swam in the gunslinger's head. Images of thirty-one dead men flooded his memories. He rarely dreamt. Particularly of those he'd killed. Conscience wasn't something he wrestled with. He was a bounty hunter—all the law that was left when the law failed. And that was justification enough for him. But tonight was different. He dreamed of all those who had drawn iron against him. But they weren't as they had been in life. They were fresh from the grave. Sunken jaws, rotting cheeks, dangling eyes, and dirty teeth from dead men's grins filled his thoughts.

The dead men cackled as they drew their guns. Flint's arms felt like they were covered in molasses; his gun stuck in a honey-filled holster.

Or was it blood? Flint felt bullets smash into his body, bursting organs and cracking limbs. His own gun finally fired. Soft bullets protruded hesitantly, then crawled across the air before snuggling up to their targets and falling harmlessly to the ground.

Flint woke with a start. His hand was already on his gun. Before him stood Hector and his dead friends.

The gunslinger shook his head, still trying to awake from his nightmare. But the scent of the fire, Hector's aura of pig, and now the stench of rotting flesh, were all too real.

"I told you, senor! I am el Diablo!"

The dead men's faces pulled tight in the hungry smile of the damned. Julio had Flint's rifle in his blood-crusted hands. Jauquin simply waddled and slobbered like some demented fiend spying easy prey.

But no one made a move.

Hector was still tied up, but standing. "The policia chased us for days, senor. Deep into the jungle. We killed too many, I think, and they wanted us dead. There were eight of us when we started, but two of my amigos died before we found the ruins. We climbed high, hoping to use our rifles to pick off some of the policia from the high pyramid in the center. Jose found a tunnel beneath the vines and went inside. He yelled for us to come in. I stayed outside on watch. I heard mi amigos shouting. Happy shouts. 'Gold!' said one. 'Emeralds!' said another. Then I heard them open something. It sounded heavy and made of stone. Then I heard them scream. They fired their guns. I heard more than a dozen shots. But whatever they found would not die. Then Antonio called on Jesus and fired his sawed-off. It was quiet inside after that. Dead quiet. I crept to the top of the pyramid and looked inside the passage. One of mi amigos was there, his throat torn out as if by el lobo. I followed the blood around the corner and saw a room full of wonders. Full of treasure, gold, lapis lazuli—even a statue of a green jaguar. Mi amigos were everywhere. Their throats had been slashed, their eyes gouged—their brains pulled right out of their broken skulls. Then I saw the mummy. It was lying on top of Antonio—he had been a priest once, before the policia killed his brother. The thing had bitten into his face, tearing out his eyes! Can you imagine, senor? Biting someone hard enough to eat out their eyes?"

Flint shook his head slowly, studying the undead things before him, but they did not yet move. His horror and revulsion gave way to his well-honed instinct for survival. There would be time enough to go insane later on.

"I started taking the best treasures, stuffing them into a sack. Then I saw a necklace around the mummy's throat. I pushed it off Antonio and tried to snap the chain, but it wouldn't break. So I kicked the mummy's head off and took if off the stump!" Hector laughed like a madman at that. His friends seemed to snicker as well.

Flint knew the things retained at least some of their brains then.

"Soon as I put the damned necklace on, these words came to me, senor. I had never heard them before, but I could speak them, and I knew what they meant. 'Ixcaret yecth atatl.' It means 'Arise from the dead!,' gringo! And chu know what? Mi amigos did just that! They stood! I tell you, I nearly pissed my pants. But they just stood there looking even more stupid than they had in life. The policia found me then. Things were different with them. My hombre muertos were unstoppable. They tore them to pieces and ATE THEIR FLESH!"

At that the two zombies struck. Julio raised the rifle and Jauquin lunged forward. Flint drew and fanned his Colt through his serape. The rounds stitched up Julio's guts but did little more than knock him back. The dead bandit's shot fared little better, passing straight through Flint's holey

serape and lodging in the baked Texas dirt. Jauquin landed in front of Flint and made to bite his outstretched leg. The gunslinger kicked him in the jaw, saw teeth shatter and fall, then fanned once more, plugging the once-dead bandit smack in the forehead and spattering Julio with his rotten brains.

The thing stopped moving. Flint would remember that.

Flint stood and fanned once more—but his pistol was empty. Stupid!, he thought to himself.

Hector cackled and Julio laughed as he sluggishly raised the rifle once more. Flint spun in his serape, avoiding the shot in the confusion. He stopped his twirl facing Julio, his second pistol in his hand. "Stay dead," he grunted as he fired one shot at Julio's forehead. The zombie's eyes crossed as they seemed to follow the shot in, then trailed inward and followed the voracious .44 caliber slug into the gray, grainy bits beyond.

"Ixcaret yecth atatl" Hector shouted, but it was too late. The brain was the key. He knew it and now Flint did too.

The gunslinger walked toward Hector and slowly lit another cigar. Then he reached down and roughly yanked the bandit's shirt open. The necklace was ugly. A contorted, screaming face surrounded by what looked like a sunburst. Flint reached down to yank the thing off, but some unseen force held it down.

Hector regained some of his composure. "I have tried, senor. But it only seems to come off when the wearer ees dead. And you need me alive. There is a bonus for recovering the bank's dinero. No?"

Flint grimaced. He looked at the twice-dead thing beside him and sneered. "Hell with the bonus."

He put a bullet through Hector's face.

## Introduction

Any survivor can handle a pack of zombies with an Uzi and a flamethrower. But what happens when the last one standing has nothing but six bullets and a belly-full of sand? That's what Westerns are all about.

The Western genre is about personal achievement. Does an hombre have the grit to stand in the middle of the street at High Noon and duel it out with the dead? The cavalry might come, but only after the fight is over. If they come any earlier, the heroes likely *are* the cavalry.

Welcome to *Fistful o' Zombies*, the Western setting book for the phenomenal *All Flesh Must Be Eaten*. Inside this book, players and the Zombie Master can find everything needed to run any type of Western, from John Wayne epics to the titular spaghetti Western to the era of the Singing Cowboys!

## The Western

So just what is a Western? That's an arguable point. Even some science fiction stories are labeled Westerns by film critics. The sci-fi classic *Outland*, for instance, is essentially a remake of Gary Cooper's *High Noon* in space. That's all well and good for those in film school, but this book is a little more literal.

Geography is a good starting point. Westerns take place in the West. Specifically, the American West— an area that stretches from California to the Mississippi. The land here ranges from the blistering deserts of the Southwest to the temperate High Plains to the freezing pine forests of the high mountains and northern territories. Alaska and Mexico also figure into many famous Western tales.

The West is also a "period." Given the huge area of the West, relatively few whites were there prior to 1900. The vast nature of the West and the relatively small numbers who first settled it made for isolated towns with little or no governmental authority. Guns made the first laws and often settled all claims. What law did come was sometimes just as crooked as the thieves it tried to corral.

Of course, whites weren't the only inhabitants of the West. Millions of Native Americans—Indians—had been there for thousands of years. Most were friendly enough, but white greed and the refusal of the Indians to be "civilized" resulted in violence almost from the start. This period—when "white" towns were scarce, government authority was lax, and Indians were still a significant force—define the West as much as its geography.

The final characteristic of the West is the people who lived there. The environment, Indians, and lack of authority made Westerners a tough lot. Most every man went "heeled," or armed, especially when away from town, and most every woman who ever rode a wagon from "Back East" knew how to handle a rifle. The toughest of the bunch often served as inspiration for the rest, and later even defined the generation. Legends such as Buffalo Bill, Wild Bill Hickok, Wyatt Earp, Doc Holliday, Annie Oakley, Calamity Jane, Jesse James and Billy the Kid were all born from the rugged individualism demanded by the unforgiving nature of the Wild West.

## History and Hollywood

The West would no doubt have been unique enough if left to pure history, but once Hollywood got involved, it became the stuff of legends. Movies about the heroes of the Wild West started even before the period had come to a close. The earliest films starred authentic Western heroes like Black Bart, with well-known figures such as Wyatt Earp as "technical advisors." A 1919 film about Custer's massacre at the Little Big Horn even featured several Indians who actually took part in the battle. Perception is reality, so it is very important to understand Hollywood's influence on the Western. Several of the settings presented in this book draw directly on sub-genres of Western films. Here's a quick primer for those who are not so well-versed in the history of Western cinema.

> ### Inspiration
>
> There are a few movies and TV shows one might find useful for inspiration and plot ideas. *The Killing Box* (sometimes labeled *The Lost Regiment*) and *Unforgiven* have some neat ideas. The remake of the *Wild, Wild West* and the original television show have lots of neat plots and gadgets for those who want to add a little steampunk to the game. One might also try *Billy the Kid Meets Dracula* for pure camp and the *Valley of Gwanji* for dinosaurs!
>
> Readers may find some books helpful as well. *Confederacy of the Dead*, *Razored Saddles*, and *Trails of Darkness* (by Robert E. Howard of *Conan* fame) are chock full of horrid tales. The award-winning *Deadlands* roleplaying game, by this book's author, also has more zombies than a cowboy has saddle sores. Rules for converting *Deadlands* characters into *All Flesh Must Be Eaten*, and vice versa, are included at the end of this book (see p. 136) or those with the notion.

The first Westerns were basically film versions of the "dime novels," where characters like Wild Bill Hickok were bigger than life. A few realistic movies were made, but the most popular featured heroes who never missed, never ran out of ammo, and never got shot. Patrons voted for heroic films with their dollars and by the 1930s, the heroes of the Westerns were goody-two-shoes in white hats. Inexplicably, they began to sing as well. Randolph Scott, Gene Autry, and Roy Rogers defined a new type of gunslinger—the "singing cowboy." These heroes never killed someone unless they had to—preferring to use their superhuman skills to shoot the guns out of the bad guys' hands when they could. They never drank or swore, and showed respect to women, children, and their elders. **Chapter Three: Singing Cowboys** explores what happens when these heroic fantasies mix with the grim world of *All Flesh Must Be Eaten*.

A new breed of Western emerged during the fifties and remained popular through the 1970s. The new cowboy was no longer as pure as his predecessors. He drank like a fish, slapped his woman when she got out of line, shot the bad guys in the guts, and would not be caught dead singing. This era belonged to John Wayne and it stayed his until his death in 1979. Other stars shared the spotlight—Gary Cooper, Charles Bronson, Burt Lancaster—but they never took it. This era is covered in **Chapter Four: True Grit**, named both for one of the Duke's classic films and for the type of hero that defines the sub-genre.

Though John Wayne remained popular in the sixties, a new type of Western emerged as well. These films were made—of all places—in Italy, by Italians. A young American named Clint Eastwood was the star. Were it not for his twitching eye and steely demeanor, the "spaghetti Westerns" might never have entered the genre. Another reason these films began to compete with classic John Wayne films was the Duke's political dedication to America's war in Vietnam. His public condemnation of those who protested the war caused idealistic youths to shun his movies. Though the effect was minimal at the box office, it gave an opening to the rebellious spaghettis. Eastwood and his director, Sergio Leone, capitalized on America's resentment of authority by making him even more of an anti-hero than John Wayne's usual character. Wayne was tough and ornery, but he was often a United States Marshal or Union officer. Eastwood's heroes were usually outlaws or former lawmen who had been wronged by authority. This played heavily on America's sensitivities during the long Vietnam War and no doubt accounted for much of Eastwood's initial popularity. Still, just as important to the films' success was their emphasis on style over detailed plots and characters. Long pauses, focus on visuals, odd music, and short "one-liners" became the spaghettis' avant-garde trademark. In the film *Once Upon a Time in the West*, eighteen minutes of movie pass before the opening credits appear! And the music of *The Good, the Bad, and the Ugly* has become synonymous with a showdown. These kinds of stories are covered in **Chapter Five: Spaghetti with Meat**.

From the 1980s to the present, Westerns have dabbled in several different styles, but no overriding theme has dominated. Some of the best—*Dances with Wolves*, *Pale Rider*, *Unforgiven*, *Tombstone* and *Ride with the Devil* were fairly realistic. *Young Guns* made Billy the Kid and his companions a contemporary "Magnificent Seven," with emphasis on action and one-liners in the grand style of the 1980s. *Silverado* did much the same. Western horror has a few entries as well, such as *Ravenous* and *The Lost Regiment*. Steampunk, anachronistic "mad science," was first introduced in the *Wild Wild West* television program of the 1960s and made a comeback with a movie version in 1999. Another television show *The Adventures of Brisco County Jr.*, featured comedy and steampunk. Joss Whedon's *Firefly* TV series is an interesting amalgam of space opera and the West.

This book allows Zombie Masters and players to join in any of these eras, styles or sub-genres. Time to saddle up, pardner.

## Chapter Summary

**Chapter One: Go West** presents these introductory remarks. The overview above should also help the Zombie Master understand the various sub-genres of Westerns.

**Chapter Two: The Good, the Bad, and the Dead** discusses the history of the West and presents information on how to create characters. Some general Archetypes may be found here, good for any Western-oriented settings. Look for additional, more setting-specific archetypes in many of the subsequent chapters.

**Chapter Three: Singing Cowboys** is the first of four detailed campaign settings. Here the Zombie Master finds guitar-strumming white hats battling pockets of undead in one of the weirdest survival-horror tales ever!

**Chapter Four: True Grit** focuses on "real men"—John Wayne-types fighting an ancient and mysterious evil.

**Chapter Five: Spaghetti with Meat** is the feature setting of this book. Stringy "men-with-no-names" pull on their serapes and strap on their six-guns to do battle with the worst kind of zombies—smart, tough, and fast on the draw.

**Chapter Six: Dances with Zombies** tells the tale from the Indian's side. What happens when the approaching "white demons" turn out to be just that? In this setting, Native American heroes learn just how hard it is to fight the palefaces' army with bows and arrows. Especially when the faces are paler than usual!

**Chapter Seven: Other Settings** covers additional ideas for tales of Western zombie horror, each presented in broad outline, to be fleshed out by individual Zombie Masters for campaign play, or used as fire-and-forget, one-shot adventures.

**Appendix** includes conversion notes for using the materials from either the Wild, Wasted or Way Out West roleplaying game, *Deadlands*, in any *All Flesh Must Be Eaten* campaign, or vice versa.

## How to Use A Fistful o' Zombies

The first two chapters in this book are for players and Zombie Masters alike. They include information on the setting and creating player characters. Players should not read beyond Chapter Two or they risk spoiling the secrets that await within those settings. The Zombie Master, however, should share some information from these chapters, such as any special rules created for the setting. The archetypes are also designed to present just enough to get the heroes going without revealing everything about the setting or the mysterious horrors that await within.

As in all *All Flesh Must Be Eaten* setting books, the Zombie Master can run adventures in the individual settings as "one-shots," or he can turn the heroes' adventures into a protracted campaign.

# Conventions

This book has different graphic features that identify the type of information presented. This text is standard text, and it is used for general explanations.

> Certain text is set off from the standard text in this manner. This is sidebar text and it contains additional, but tangential information, or supplemental charts and tables.

> Other text is set apart in this way. It details Supporting Cast or Adversaries that may be used in Stories at the Zombie Master's discretion.

## Dice Notations

D10, D8, D6 and D4 mean a ten-sided die, an eight-sided die, a six-sided die and a four-sided die, respectively. When a number appears before the notation, that number of such dice should be rolled and their results should be added together. For example, 2D6 means roll two six-sided dice, and generate a result between 2 and 12. Multipliers are expressed after the dice notation. For example, 3D10 x 4 means roll three ten-sided dice, add the results together, and multiply that total result by 4. This generates a number between 12 and 120. A number in parentheses after, or in the middle of, the notation is the average roll. This number is provided for those that want to avoid dice rolling and just get the result. So the notation D6 x 4(12) means that players who want to skip rolling just use the value 12. Some notations cannot provide a set number because their result depends on a variable factor. For example, D8(4) x Strength is used because the Strength value to be plugged into that notation will vary depending on who is acting.

## Gender

Every roleplaying game struggles with the decision about third person pronouns and possessives. While the male reference (he, him, his) is customarily used for both male and female, there is no question that it is not entirely inclusive. On the other hand, the "he or she" structure is clumsy and unattractive. In an effort to "split the difference," this book uses male designations for even chapters and female designations for odd chapters.

## Measurements

This book primarily uses U.S. measurements (feet, yards, miles, pounds, etc.). Metric system equivalents appear in parentheses. In the interests of ease of use, the conversions are rounded relatively arbitrarily. For example, miles are multiplied by 1.5 to get kilometers (instead of 1.609), meters are equal to yards (instead of 1.094 yards), pounds are halved to get kilograms (instead of multiplied by 0.4536), and so on. If a Zombie Master feels that more precision is necessary, she should take the U.S. measurements provided and apply more exact formulas.

## Lexicon

**Adios:** Spanish for "goodbye."

**Arbuckle's:** A famous brand of coffee that became synonymous with coffee itself.

**Beeve:** A Texas longhorn. The word itself is a bastardized plural form of "beef."

**Billy Yank:** A Federal soldier.

**Bluebelly:** A Federal soldier (because of their blue uniforms).

**Britches:** Pants.

**Buffalo:** Hit someone over the head with a pistol butt. Wyatt Earp was known for buffaloing troublemakers.

**Derringer:** A small one or two-shot weapon originally invented by Henry Deringer. Later imitators were called "Derringers" to avoid trademark violations. Both spellings were used interchangeably, but properly, only those guns manufactured by Henry Deringer were spelled in his namesake. The rest are collectively labeled "derringers," though even these were often capitalized as if named after the creator.

**Hanging Judge:** A judge known to hang convicted criminals. Judge Roy Bean is the most famous of these.

**Hogleg:** Pistol.

**Hoosegow:** Jail.

**Hurrah:** Cattlemen often "hurrahed," or intimidated a town by riding up and down its streets, firing their guns into the air, in shop windows, and so on.

**Iron Horse:** A train.

**Johnny Reb:** A Confederate soldier.

**Law Dog:** A lawman.

**Lead Poisoning:** To die of gunshot wounds.

**Lynch Mob:** A group of citizens who decides someone is guilty of a crime and hangs them without benefit of a trial.

**Necktie Party:** A hanging by a lynch mob.

**Paleface:** A "Hollywood Indian" name for a white person.

**Posse:** A group of citizens temporarily hired or empowered to chase down a criminal.

**Red Man:** An Indian.

**Repeater:** A repeating rifle, such as the famous Winchester '76.

**Rimrocking:** Driving sheep off a cliff to their death (often done by cattlemen to sheepfarmers' herds).

**Six-gun:** A revolving pistol (most could hold six shots).

**Smokewagon:** Pistol.

**Street Howitzer:** A double-barreled shotgun.

**Tinhorn (or greenhorn):** An inexperienced person, usually from Back East.

## About the Author

Shane Lacy Hensley's first published work was *The Temple of Rec Stalek* for West End Games' TORG line. He went on to write three novels, assisted with a handful of computer games, and designed over 50 game books for such companies as White Wolf, TSR, SSI, and FASA. In 1996, he founded Pinnacle Entertainment Group and wrote the award-winning *Deadlands*. *Fistful o' Zombies* is his first freelance work since he started Pinnacle.

Shane lives in Blacksburg, Virginia, with his wife, Michelle, and his little rustlers Caden and Ronan. His two dogs, Feebee and Roadkill (you can guess which one he named) prowl the High Plains around his house.

# CHAPTER TWO

# THE GOOD, THE BAD, AND THE DEAD

"Never thought it'd end like this."

"Nope."

"Always thought some whore'd gimme a disease I couldn't cut off."

"Yup."

"I'm hungry, Pete." Burke sliced off a piece of his saddle, stuck it on the end of his knife, and held it in the small fire. The smoke rose through the hole in the cabin's roof. The cold here in Truckee Pass was brutal—one of the worst the area had ever seen. But the cold wasn't about to kill Pete or Burke—two trappers who'd thrown in with a bunch of settlers from Back East for safety. It was the rest of Donner's crew that was the real danger. They'd gone blood-simple with hunger. It started with their Indian guide. They had brained him, chopped him up like squirrel, and passed his red meat around the circle like it was Sunday dinner. "Just a red man," Donner had said. "No harm done." Then the old woman had died. Someone said it was the cold. Cooked and ate her too.

The leather was as soft as it was going to be. Burke pulled it out of the fire, blew on it a bit, then took a tentative bite. The hot saddle burned his lips. Pete looked over suddenly. Had he smelled the cooking flesh of his friend's mouth? Nah, that's crazy, thought Burke.

Pete cocked his flintlock pistol. Burke covered his mouth, his paranoia growing. "What is it?"

"Heard sumthin'." The dirty trapper still had the old woman's blood in his blonde beard. "Sumthin's diggin' around outside."

"That's impossible. Snow's completely covered the cabin. Gotta be ten feet high out there!" Burke muttered, though he heard it now too.

"We got guns in here! An' plenty o' powder. So just go on and dig somewhere else! Ain't no meat in here for you." He repeated it again, this time in Ute. Just in case.

A log midway up the south wall of the cabin began to wiggle. Snow fell in wet clumps to the floor. After a bit, the wood tumbled in after it. Pete stood and aimed his pistol at the hole. "Get outta here!" he screamed.

Burke cowered in the corner and reached for his musket. "What is it? A bear?"

"Ain't no bear," Pete growled.

Suddenly a half-frozen face and a bloody arm shot through the hole. Pete felt his blood freeze.

"The Injun!" Burke screamed.

"Can't be the Injun," Pete yelled back. "We et half of him!"

The grim figure pushed itself further in. Snow covered much of its flesh, but what was exposed had long, neat strips cut right off the bone.

"It's the Injun," Burke sobbed quietly. He crawled backward into the corner and cocked his musket.

"We'll shoot you, red man!" Pete growled, but the dead Indian did not stop tunneling through the cabin wall.

"I knew better. Knew better'n ta eat someone. Even a Injun," Burke babbled.

Pete heard him cock his musket. "Shoot him, Burke!" he screamed. There was a single shot, but Pete saw nothing. He whirled and saw a red stain that had been Burke's head. His smoking musket lay between his twitching legs.

"God damn you for a coward," Pete said.

# The Weird West

The "West" is more an era than it is a place. Obviously, the vast majority of tales actually take place in the American West (from the Mississippi to the west coast). But there are plenty of "Westerns" that can take place elsewhere as well. The haunted "hollers" of Kentucky, the Lovecraftian hills of New England, or even the industrialized cities of Los Angeles or Chicago can become settings for Western Horror. This book does not concentrate on these places though. *Fistful o' Zombies* focuses on the more stereotypical boomtowns, wide open prairies, and lonely deserts of the true West. A Zombie Master with a great idea for an adventure that takes place in New York City should not be scared off, however. There is more than enough information included to accommodate any tale that takes place within this era.

Chronologically, there are three distinct eras of the West: the Old West, Wild West, and New West. The settings in this book mostly take place in the Wild West, where the most familiar weapons and technology exist. Should a Zombie Master want to place a story in the Old or New West, the sections below provide him a brief sense of history. He and the players can also check the weapons tables (see pp. 34-35) to see when particular guns were introduced. That can be very important as certain advancements in firearms were directly responsible for "taming" the West. Fighting zombies with black powder weapons, for example, is much harder than fighting them with repeating Winchesters and Gatling guns.

## The Old West

The Old West starts about 1830 and runs through the the end of the Civil War. This period features small bands of whites entirely outnumbered by Indians, with nothing but black powder weapons to fight them . . . and whatever other horrors exist in the dark, unexplored frontier.

Those few who ventured this far from civilization are truly on their own. No area is truly settled and even forts are few and far between. Those forts that do exist may house little more than a platoon (roughly twenty horsemen). A party that finds itself attacked by hostiles must handle it on its own. Even worse, the sick and injured had better hope for a quick death as the nearest doctor is likely more than a month and several unforgiving mountain ranges away.

White men first came to the West to explore, and soon after, to trap. The lucrative trade in beaver, raccoon, fox, bear, mink, ermine, and other game pelts called forth a strong breed of predominantly French and English trappers. These hunters traveled alone or in small groups of two or three, venturing into the vast unknown and outnumbered by a strange and sometimes savage people. Greed and paranoia are common. Tales of trappers killing their mates at the end of the season for pelts are just as common. Trappers heading into the hills in spring would often come across the thawing bodies of the betrayed from the winter before.

Given the nature of single-shot muskets and Indian relations at this time, surviving even a small outbreak of the dead becomes a major issue.

## The Wild West

The end of the American Civil War changed the West dramatically. The years between 1865 and 1900 mark the period known as the Wild West in *All Flesh Must Be Eaten*.

The first change was technological. Repeating pistols and revolvers become common, allowing whites to fight off their Indian foes even when outnumbered. Even more importantly, millions of dispossessed whites moved West. Most were soldiers who found themselves unemployed after the end of the "War Between the States." Others had their homes destroyed by the war or perhaps lost their families in the long conflict. Millions of freed slaves also made the trek West, looking for new lives away from the Jim Crow laws of the South and the patronizing ambivalence of the North.

This is the classic Western period. Legends like Buffalo Bill and Wild Bill Hickok became famous and gave the West its "outlaw" prestige, mostly thanks to the wild success of dime novels exaggerating or outright inventing their incredible lives. The famous "Shootout at the OK Corral" occurred during this era too, exemplifying the public's conception of the Wild West.

Any player who has ever watched a Western is likely familiar with the accents, the technology, and the scenery of the Wild West.

## The New West

The New West covers the turn of the century up through 1930 or so. The Indian threat is over, but small-town corruption and bank robbers still plague the land. Horseless carriages and early motorcycles become the new mounts of choice, and Peacemakers are replaced by Colt Automatics. Still, the men and women who live here are the tough, stoic cowboys of legend. *All Flesh Must Be Eaten* adventures set in this time offer an interesting mix of technology with traditional Western trappings. Small towns still have rowdy saloons, boom towns still rise up whenever gold or silver is found, and train robbers still prowl the outlands—though they might chase trains with the latest Model T.

In the 1920s, when Prohibition rears its head, a booze-running (or anti-booze-running) campaign set in the western outlands might also be interesting, especially if a bad batch of "hooch" causes a zombie outbreak.

## History of the West

Running a game in a relatively unfamiliar time period can be quite difficult. The following section should help Zombie Masters understand the events surrounding their campaign, and aid players in creating backstories for their characters.

## The Gold Rush

In 1848, a large vein of gold was discovered at Sutter's Mill in California. The next year, nearly 30,000 settlers rushed to the coast to get their share. The 2000-mile trip was difficult, with chronic diseases, food shortages, and hostile Indians dogging their every mile. A popular saying at the time was that the "cowards never started and the weak died on the way."

The impact of the Gold Rush cannot be overstated. In the wake of these tough survivors came a tidal wave of brothels, provisioners, and perhaps most numerous—saloons. The boom was not limited to the coast, either. Hundreds of towns along the most heavily traveled routes from East to West became supply depots for California-bound settlers. The Mormons in Salt Lake City also benefited from frequent travelers who found their city on the way, though the Saints were at first reluctant to serve transient "gentiles" with gold fever.

## The Donner Party

One of the most unfortunate groups of settlers headed West was led by George Donner. The leader and others were convinced to try an untested route by an erroneous book, *The Emigrant's Guide to Oregon and California* by Lansford Hastings. They made Truckee Pass, California by Halloween, but a terrible snowstorm kept them from going any further. Most of the party of 81 scattered between the pass and Alder's Creek five miles back. Terrible blizzards kept the groups isolated and without food or supplies. As the weakest began to die, the starving settlers resorted to cannibalism. Only two killings occurred, both of which could be called euthanasia. Popular folklore says otherwise. According to the most lurid stories, the settlers quickly turned on the weak, killing them and eating their flesh. In the worlds of *All Flesh Must Be Eaten*, this is almost certainly the case. For more tales of survival in extreme conditions with the added threat of zombies, see "North, to Alaska" in Chapter Seven: Other Settings.

## The Mexican-American War

Texas spirit may be an icon of America these days, but it was not always so. Texans were almost universally reviled by most Westerners as bad men and troublemakers. It is no surprise that Texas' troubles with Mexico gave most Americans little reason for concern. The first invasion of Texas by General Antonio Lopez de Santa Anna was all but ignored by the rest of the country. The refusal of Santa Anna to accept quarter (no prisoners) was likely what began changing American minds. This happened first at San Jocinto, then at the famous Alamo (where legendary Americans like Davy Crockett, Sam Bowie and Sam Houston were killed). The "Texas rebellion," as Santa Anna put it, was over too fast for America to become involved, but they would "remember the Alamo" ten years later when Texas officially joined the Union and Santa Anna marched north again.

This time, the United States and Mexico officially went to war. In a short and brilliant campaign (1846-1848), the U.S. defeated Santa Anna's army and carried the war all the way to Mexico City. Perhaps just as important, a whole generation of American Army officers received their baptism of fire. These men would later go on to lead the largest bloodletting in U.S. history—the American Civil War (more on that in a bit). The war also gave birth to the Texas Rangers and repeating revolvers.

## The American Civil War

In 1861, South Carolina seceded from the United States (the Union). The men who instigated this separation believed the federal government had grown too large and authoritarian and wanted to see a return to "states' rights." Slavery, in particular, was at issue. The South depended heavily on cheap labor for the arduous and demanding job of picking cotton. The North had no such need and thus could afford to be more altruistic.

Southern—Confederate—forces issued a proclamation that U.S. forces leave southern soil. The Federals did not. So, the opening salvo of the war was fired on Fort Sumter in Charleston Harbor on April 12th. By July of that year, the butternut and gray-clad Confederate Army faced the bluebellied Federal troops at Manassas, Virginia. The first Battle of Bull Run ended in a pathetic Union rout and encouraged the rebels to stage what would become a far longer war than anyone had imagined at the time.

Unfortunately, both armies at first attempted to use traditional "line and column" tactics, the same formations used in the American Revolutionary War a hundred years earlier, and even the Napoleonic Wars of the early 1800s. Few realized that the improvement of modern arms (particularly in the more accurate rifled muskets) and the mass production of cannons and ammunition made such tactics suicidal. The military leadership was slow to learn, but by the end of the war, the American East foreshadowed the Great War of 1914. Trenches crisscrossed the once-pristine Virginia wilderness, and repeating rifles made a company of men equal to a battalion armed with muskets. The industrial age transformed warfare and over 600,000 Americans died to prove it.

The details of the Civil War are far too numerous to recite here, but several books and films are available for those who need more background. The best books are likely too involved for the high action desired in a roleplaying game, but the Shelby Foote series is excellent. For a quicker fix, particularly good films are *Glory, Gettysburg,* and *Ride with the Devil.* One of the more interesting tales of the war is featured in the Turner film, *The Hunley,* about the South's experimental submarine (raised in 2000, incidentally). *Andersonville,* another Turner film, is also a great look at the deplorable conditions and outright horror of the war's prison camps (and the inmates even look like zombies by the end of the film).

The end of the war left a scarred nation brewing with trouble. Hatred for those who had killed kith and kin was remembered long after General Robert E. Lee signed the final peace treaty at Appomattox, Virginia in 1865. Local hostilities between Northerners and Southerners lasted for over a century thereafter.

## Slavery

Slavery was abolished by the Emancipation Proclamation in 1863, and applied to the Confederate States upon their surrender. Unfortunately for most blacks, their former masters had not educated them, and little help toward integrating into society would come from local or federal authorities. Many of the freed slaves headed West where they could put their limited skills to work on their own isolated homesteads. One of the greatest secrets of the West is just how many black cowboys there were. The Mario van Peebles film *Posse* is an interesting look at an entire town of dispossessed blacks attempting to start a new way of life.

## End of Hostilities

The second rush West began with the end of the Civil War. Hundreds of thousands of soldiers and support personnel (uniform makers, arms makers and so on) suddenly found themselves out of work. Hundreds of thousands of newly freed slaves headed West to find new lives far away from the hostilities they found in both the North and the South. Fortunately for all, the American government made land in the West cheap for those willing to travel there and claim it. Unfortunately, the end of the conflict in the East seemed only to give rise to isolated pockets of violence in the West. A few of the bloodiest fights took place between dispossessed or bitter settlers, but most occurred between whites tried in fire back East and the various Indian tribes they came across.

## The Indian Wars

The so-called Indian Wars are a very complicated subject. For one thing, there was never a significant Indian "war." There were thousands of skirmishes and a few campaigns, such as the Nez Perce pursuit and Custer's doomed raid on the Sioux.

Revisionist historians have painted the Indian Wars as a constant battle between noble savages with murderous white men. As with most things in life, the truth is far more complicated. The Indians, for instance, were a very diverse group of people. Few fit the unreasonable ideal of the noble savage who respected the land and its bounties. Just like whites, blacks, and all other races of the earth, Indians did wonderful things—and they did horrible things. They massacred rival tribes to secure their own hunting grounds, to take new wives, or simply to mature their braves. They raped women, slaughtered children, and enslaved their foes.

Perhaps one of the reasons the Indian Wars became so vicious was that the very methods used by many of the Plains Indians were abhorrent to the soldiers who fought them. Most Indians were raiders.

Thievery, rape, and murder were side effects of their strategies. Whites did not generally involve non-combatants and felt the "red savages" should fight in lines and columns like the rest of the civilized world. This simply did not fit the Indian mentality, nor the reality of his situation. Outgunned, with no experience in such warfare, with no way of besieging Federal forts and with generally far fewer braves to "waste" in set-piece battles, Indians were forced to hit much easier targets, such as outlying settlements and isolated wagon-trains. The natives rarely stood their ground even when the occasional warband was caught, preferring to run and strike at settlers elsewhere. Whites regarded this as cowardly and took out their anger on their foes when they were able.

Perhaps most unfortunate were the non-combatants who found themselves caught up in the Indian Wars. Countless settlers paid for every treaty violation or acre of stolen land and peaceful Indians like Chief Joseph's Nez Perce were often the targets of the Army's retribution. Those Indians known to be guilty of the most savage crimes often simply returned to their villages after the deed, forcing their pursuers to battle the entire settlement just to arrest the braves responsible for raiding.

The Indian Wars were sad, violent, brutal, and sometimes nonsensical affairs. Every act of violence, like the horrible Sand Creek Massacre in 1864, where scores of Indian women and children were slaughtered, begat a wave of revenge. The great gathering of Sioux in 1876 was a direct response to white atrocities, and led to the death of General Custer and most of the 7th Cavalry Regiment.

## The Bureau of Indian Affairs

One of the most corrupt agencies in American history was the Bureau of Indian Affairs. Established in 1824, this organization sent agents into the field to negotiate peaceful terms with the Indian tribes. Agents frequently arranged to sell goods to the Indians, but often charged the tribes twice the usual price and delivered half the goods, selling the rest for themselves. Agents were also known to have sold blankets infected with fatal diseases (such as smallpox or dysentery) to the tribes, sometimes wiping out scores of innocents out of pure malice. Sometimes agents even acted with local militia, drawing a tribe's braves to a meeting while other whites attacked their villages. As a rule, Indian agents were not good people. Those who were often found themselves overwhelmed as they made promises quickly broken by other whites. With little authority, most good agents quit in disgust, leaving the doors wide open for those looking for profit or pure meanness.

The Bureau was transferred to the Department of the Interior in 1849, but remained plagued by corruption well into the next century. Some claim the agency remains a pawn of special interests to date.

## Buffalo Soldiers

"Buffalo Soldiers" were black soldiers inducted into the United States Army after the war. They fought mostly out West against the Indians, who called them "Buffalo Soldiers" because of their wooly hair and black skin. These regiments fought hard and well, even though many of their white officers—some former Southern officers—held them in contempt.

There were only two official Buffalo Soldier regiments, the 9th and 10th cavalry. Both were created in 1866 and featured large numbers of veterans from the Civil War. They played major roles in the taming of the West, most notably by fighting the Apaches. Perhaps more importantly, but less exciting, Buffalo Soldiers strung thousands of miles of telegraph wires, mapped unexplored territory and protected mail routes.

## Iron Horses

In 1862, President Lincoln authorized the building of a transcontinental railroad by two companies, the Central Pacific in the West and the Union Pacific in the East. Both railroads almost failed due to financial mismanagement during the Civil War, but took off again afterwards as those made wealthy by the war looked for new investments. Labor was also cheap as thousands of soldiers were released from service with no immediate employment.

The transcontinental railroad was completed on May 10th, 1869 at Promontory Point in northern Utah. President Grant himself drove the last "golden spike" linking the lines.

The trip from the Mississippi River to California typically took about four days. Getting from various stops along the route to one's true destination occurred by horse, stage, or even on foot.

"Iron horses" transformed the West from Old to Wild as more and more people traveled the lines to the frontier. The rails also ushered in a whole new age of corruption. Unscrupulous individuals often had inside knowledge of where new "spurs" would be laid, making the land and towns along them far more valuable. These men would then snatch up the land for what seemed a generous price, then resell it after the rail line was built for tremendous profit. When settlers did not want to move, they were often "persuaded" by any means necessary.

The competition between rail companies was fierce. "Rail wars" often broke out between rivals. Gangs of well-armed men would raid other companies' camps and attempt to drive off their work crews, steal their equipment, or sabotage their lines. The violence became so bad in some spots that the U.S. Army was called in to keep the peace.

Most importantly, the railroads spelled the doom of the remaining Native Americans. Settlers and the army itself could quickly move around the country, then mount up to strike Indians suspected of raiding. Worse still for the natives, the railroads simply brought more and more people each year. As they spread, so did contact with Indians and this almost always led to trouble. Whites who saw valuable land, especially deposits of gold or silver, squatted on Indian lands regardless of treaties or laws passed by the government. When the Indians attempted to fight back (usually with particularly brutal methods), the army was called out to hang the troublemakers and chase off the rest until new reservations could be found.

## Cattle

Longhorn steers raised in Texas were big business after the Civil War. These animals were tough and rangy, but their ability to survive on sparse prairie grass made their stringy meat more than welcome to settlers far from the meat markets of the East. Financially, the longhorns were a major success because the vast majority of cattlemen allowed their animals to "free range" on the open plains. This meant they could feed and "house" the animals for free, then sell them at great profit. When cattlemen were forced to buy the land their animals grazed on, the era of the cattle kings ended.

At the height of the cattle trade, steers were driven from all over Texas up through several trails, including the Chisholm, Shawnee, and Goodnight-Loving. Their destinations were railheads established in Colorado, Missouri, and primarily Kansas. Scores of new boomtowns, like legendary Dodge City, sprang up because of the cattle drives. These towns were especially violent after the cattle drivers arrived. These men had been on the trail for weeks. They were grimy, dusty, thirsty, and randy. A little whiskey usually turned into a lot of whiskey, transforming normally quiet cowboys into rowdy mobs of armed gunslingers.

Ranch hands looked forward to hitting town because cattle drives were such difficult work. The vast herds churned up tons of earth, most of which settled in a cowboy's clothes, eyes, and lungs. Also, longhorns are ornery animals, prone to turn on their drivers and gore them or their horses. Indians, rustlers, outlaws, rival drivers, and shady companions made these long treks dangerous and unpredictable. Tense and tired, ranch hands often went wild when paid up and released on some town along their path. Saloon owners and brothels eagerly anticipated the cattlemen's money, but knew the risks they ran when these wild cowboys "hurrahed" their towns.

These rowdy men were the primary reason towns like Wichita and Dodge instituted "No Firearms" policies. Drunken cattlemen would fight even if both hands were tied behind their backs, but without guns, most disputes were not fatal. Wyatt Earp was a major proponent of "No Firearms" laws. Primarily because of this law, Wyatt Earp, the most famous of the boomtown lawmen, never fired a shot at a cowboy until the famous incident near the OK Corral.

## Cattlemen and Sheepherders

Another source of violence in the Wild West was the constant war between sheepherders and cattlemen. Sheep are a particularly messy herd animal and their waste was rumored to be intolerable to steers. It did not help that by the time sheep became popular in the West, the cattlemen already possessed most of the land. Much of the land where the trouble took place, however, was still owned by the government. Cattlemen had claimed for years that such land was "free range," giving them the right to feed their herds there. When the sheepherders moved in, however, the cattlemen changed their tune.

The sheepherders used the cattlemen's own arguments against them, claiming they had just as much right to the verdant, unclaimed "free range" pastures as anyone. The cattle barons had no real argument and so often turned to bullying or violence instead. Many delineated "deadlines" warned that if the sheep or their shepherds crossed those lines, they would be killed. Violence erupted early and often. Sheep were dynamited, driven off cliffs (called "rimrocking") or into quicksand, or simply shot, clubbed and otherwise killed.

The coming of barbed wire (1874) intensified the wars at first. The cattle kings put it up where and how they wanted, even crossing public roads at times. Outraged citizens and sheepherders held wire-cutting "parties" in the dead of night. As law and order came to the West and longhorns became less profitable, the violence slowed, but isolated incidents continued well into the 20th century.

# The Law

Law in the West was a fickle thing, though it can be argued it had certain merits over today's convoluted legal system. States had fairly comprehensive and complex legal traditions and rulings, but most territories had only a few general principles to guide the judges who operated on the frontier.

There are two sides in an American court case—the plaintiff and the defendant. In a criminal case, the law is the plaintiff and the accused is the defendant. A person arrested for a crime was thrown in the closest jail cell. Prisoners with longer terms were sent to one of the few larger Federal prisons like Yuma or Leavenworth. For non-violent crimes or if the judge was convinced the accused would not flee from justice, bail was usually set from $25 to $100 and the person was released, though he was politely asked not to leave town before his court date. If the accused was known to be part of a large and powerful gang or if the locals were likely to form a lynch mob, he might be moved to a more secure prison in a larger town.

In civilized courts back East, a person was innocent until proven guilty and must be proven guilty beyond a reasonable doubt (not beyond a "shadow of a doubt"). On the frontier, if the Sheriff said someone was guilty of a crime and had the slightest bit of evidence, it was often enough to get a conviction. The reputation of a person counted for a lot as well. A regular church-goer who was kind to his neighbors would not likely get convicted for bank robbery just because the money was found on his ranch. An out-of-towner who looked like the bank robber might well find himself at the end of a rope, however, even if no "hard" evidence was found.

Most judges on the frontier were reasonable men with decent judgment if not full knowledge of the law. This often worked for the side of the righteous as convincing evidence was hard to come by (this was prior to the implementation of forensic science or fingerprinting). On the other hand, it was nearly impossible for the guilty to escape via legal loopholes—fancy-talking lawyers were more likely wind up with their neck in the loophole of a noose if they angered the judge or jury with picky technicalities.

## Crime and Punishment

Sentences in territories depend entirely on the whim of the Judge,
but here are a few common offenses and sentences for guidance.

| Offense | Sentence |
|---------|----------|
| Horse Thieving | Hanging |
| Rustling | Hanging |
| Murder | Hanging |
| Rape | Hanging |
| Attempted Murder | 20+ years or Hanging |
| Bank Robbing | 20+ years |
| Train Robbing | 20+ years |
| Stealing from a Widow | 20+ years |
| Thievery | 5 years or more for goods worth more than $300 |
| Thievery | 1 week to 5 years for goods worth less than $300 |

Most large towns had a full-time judge, but small towns in isolated locales had to wait on "circuit judges" who literally made a circuit of the small towns under their jurisdiction.

"Hanging judges" were those who had a reputation for being severe in their sentencing. They were not necessarily crooked, but they did tend to be quicker in their judgments than those who had not developed such a reputation. If a party goes before a hanging judge, they had best find some evidence to prove their innocence fast.

## Law Men

The enforcers of the law were usually hardy souls trying to bring a little order to the rough frontier.

Town Marshals enforced the law within town limits. Though these men are commonly called "marshals," do not confuse them with actual "U.S. Marshals."

Sheriffs are the law in the county. They act in place of Town Marshals only if a particular locale did not have a lawman of its own. In most states and territories, there was no clear "chain of command" between county and town law officers. The rule of will was in effect when lawmen clash. In Tombstone prior to the famous "Shootout at the OK Corral," town law under Fred White and later Virgil Earp usually sided with Wyatt Earp and his brothers. County law, under Sheriff John Behan, was strictly in the Clantons' "Cowboy" camp.

United States Marshals had jurisdiction throughout the states and territories. These were usually the toughest of the bunch, for they often worked alone against the most desperate outlaws on the frontier. When help was needed, Marshals enlisted local law enforcement agents who had to comply with federal law. Those who did not were often deposed unless they received special favor from the state government or other friends in high places.

Deputy Marshals were hired assistants to U.S. Marshals. Many held other jobs and performed as Deputy Marshals only when needed. Others were more or less full-timers attached to U.S. Marshals in particularly rough areas (such as Texas).

During the Civil War, U.S. Marshals still traveled south of the border in the West, but not in the East. Their jobs were made much harder however, as any outlaw who shot a few Union men (no matter how many other innocents he had shot) could then rely on the rebellious populace to help him hide and hinder any official efforts to catch him.

## Calling the Cavalry

Throughout the period, the United States Army maintained a presence in the West. Isolated garrisons containing under-strength regiments were the norm, with only a few major forts hosting entire brigades.

For those not familiar with the organization of the U.S. Army at the time, the battle groups and ranks are listed in the sidebar. Note that these commands were rarely up to full strength or organized properly. In theory, for example, a company should have around one hundred men. Desertion, sickness, garrison duty or simple lack of need kept most companies (and cavalry troops) between fifty and eighty effectives. Typical strengths are listed rather than full "paper" strengths.

### U.S. Army Battle Groups

| Unit | Men |
| --- | --- |
| Platoon | 20 Privates, 2 Corporals, and 1 Sergeant |
| Company (Cavalry Troop) | 50-60 Privates, 4 Corporals, 2 Sergeants, 1 1st Sergeant, 1 2nd or 1st Lieutenant |
| Battalion | 2 Companies, led by a Captain or a Major |
| Regiment | 2 Battalions, led by a Lieutenant Colonel or Colonel |
| Brigade | 2 or more Regiments led by a Brigadier General |
| Division | 2 or more Brigades led by a Major General |
| Corps | 2 or more Divisions led by a Lieutenant General |
| Army | 2 or more Corps led by a General |

### U.S. Army Ranks

**Enlisted**

Private

**Non-Commissioned Officers (NCOs)**

Corporal
Sergeant
1st Sergeant
Ordnance-Sergeant
Quartermaster-Sergeant
Sergeant Major

**Commissioned Officers**

2nd Lieutenant
1st Lieutenant
Captain
Major
Lieutenant Colonel
Colonel
Brigadier General
Major General
Lieutenant General
General

**Brevet:** A "brevet" rank is an honorary promotion to that rank. It was awarded usually for temporary duty beyond an officer's regularly established rank. When the mission was over, the "brevet" was usually removed and the officer reinstated at his traditional rank (typically one step lower but sometimes much more or less). Custer, for example, was officially a Lieutenant Colonel, but was "breveted" to Major General, a leap of three entire ranks! Custer usually referred to himself as "General Custer" after that, at least to those outside the military who would be unlikely to call him on the boast.

Cavalry troopers were armed with Spencer Carbines throughout most of the period, while officers carried sabers and revolvers. Infantry soldiers were equipped with Springfield muskets before repeating rifles became available. Even in 1876, when such weapons were common, soldiers of the 7th Cavalry carried Spencers (while many of their Sioux opponents held 17-shot repeating Winchesters). See pp. 34-38 for details on firearms of the period.

## Western Heroes

While the Norm Character Type may be used for Stories in *Fistful o' Zombies*, most Western Heroes should use the Survivor Character Type. Unless a particular setting in this book says otherwise, Western Cast Members may not take any Supernatural Qualities or Drawbacks.

Several Norm Archetypes appropriate for any Western-setting Story have been included at the end of this chapter. They are primarily intended for Supporting Cast Members or minor Adversaries. Still, if the players want to use them as Cast Members, best of luck to them. Survivor Archetypes specific to individual settings are located in the remaining chapters of the book.

### Modified Qualities and Drawbacks

**Addiction:** The only change to this Drawback is that most of the drugs on the list have not been invented yet. Alcohol is very common and treated as usual. Opium, laudanum, and lithium are also abused. Treat these as four-point addictions. Peyote is not particularly addictive, though it causes hallucinations and thus can be very debilitating.

**Delusions (Prejudice):** An additional prejudice comes into play in certain periods—intolerance of Northerns or Southerners. This most often occurred during and after the Civil War, but can be found up to a decade beforehand as well. For one point, a bigoted character simply dislikes those from across the "Mason-Dixon" line. He will poke and prod at them occasionally but does not do any real harm. For three points, he will work with his enemy only under duress and will not hesitate to double-cross an opponent given half a chance.

An additional level of this Drawback is available at the Zombie Master's discretion. For five points, an intolerant character will not work with his hated foe under any but the most life-threatening and immediate circumstances. If the bigot has the temperament and can get away with it, violence is an option. During the Civil War, of course, this might be excused depending on the circumstances. At all other times, murder is still a crime, though local law enforcement might be lax in their duties in particular circumstances.

Some characters might also be murderously bigoted toward Indians, blacks, or whites, at the Zombie Master's discretion and given a strong enough character background.

**Minority:** Asians, blacks, Indians and Mexicans are treated better out West than back East. Still, occasional intolerance and blatant bigotry by those in positions of power make this Drawback worth three points. The Zombie Master should ignore this penalty—or perhaps reduce it to one—if others of the same race usually surround the heroes. A Mexican in Mexico, for instance, faces no intolerance from fellow Mexicans. In fact, in Mexico, Yankee gringos suffer the intolerance.

**Resources:** Prices are much less in the West than they are in the 20th century. Reduce all the monetary amounts under resources to 5% of the amount listed. A Cast Member with miserable Resources, for example has about $5 in possessions.

**Status:** Characters with +10 or more in Status probably have dime novels written about them (if they are adventurous types). Fast-talkers are likely in a position to run for a state or territorial office. An Indian with high status is likely a chief or a respected medicine man.

### New Qualities

The following Qualities can be added to any *Fistful o' Zombies* Story.

#### Fast as Hell
**1-point Physical Quality**

A character with this Quality is incredibly fast on the draw. He gains +3 bonus to his Initiative total whenever he takes part in a showdown (see p. 33) or the first time he draws his pistol in a firefight.

This Quality is called "Fast as Heck" in the Singing Cowboys setting (see pp. 44-63). Profanity is not appropriate for these white-hatted heroes.

### Number One with a Bullet
#### 1-point Physical Quality

There are many good shots in the various settings of *All Flesh Must Be Eaten*, but few compare to Western heroes who can shoot the guns out of their opponents' hands, hit tin cans multiple times as they fly in the air and punch daylight through the rotting skulls of six zombies in one fast fan of the hammer.

A Cast Member with the Number One with a Bullet Quality halves the penalty for called shots. This doesn't affect penalties for range, environment, wounds, or other ill-effects—only the penalty for calling a shot. Shooting a charging zombie in the skull, for instance, still incurs the normal penalties for range, but the head shot, which normally has a penalty of -4, is only a -2 for a character who's Number One with a Bullet. Using the penalties provided on the Targeting Body Parts Table (see *AFMBE*, p. 104) as guidance, the Zombie Master should assign a normal penalty for other types of "trick shots" (and then halve the penalty for those who are Number One).

### Starting Funds

Cast Members in *Fistful o' Zombies* start with $50. This buys a gun and some ammo with a few bucks left for the local saloon. The Zombie Master may allow each character to have a horse if it facilitates the campaign.

### Restricted Skills

Most high-tech skills are off-limits to Western Cast Members, including Computers, Computer Hacking, Computer Programming, Electronic Surveillance, and Electronics.

Some skills are altered slightly. Driving, for instance, covers the ability to drive any sort of horse-drawn wagon, stagecoach, or team. Riding an individual horse is covered by the Riding Skill as usual.

### New Rules

Normal **Unisystem** rules work great for Western firefights. The special weapons of the time require only a few additional considerations.

### Fanning

One of the most important things to understand about Western revolvers is that they were made in single- and double-action. A double-action revolver means that pulling the trigger conducts two actions: it cocks the hammer, then releases it (allowing it to fall on the cartridge and detonate the shell, which propels the round out of the pistol). A single-action pistol means that pulling the trigger conducts only one action: it releases the hammer. The hammer has to be cocked separately, usually with the thumb.

While the double-action is normally superior to the single—it is faster and safer—a single-action revolver allows its user to "fan the hammer." This is done by holding down the trigger and smacking the hammer repeatedly with the palm of the other hand. A competent gunslinger can fire all six shots in a standard revolver in less than two seconds. These shots are very inaccurate, but in close quarters, unleashing that much lead can wreak havoc. To simulate this in the game, a character with a single-action revolver can fan one to six bullets as a single attack. These bullets can be directed at a like number of targets (or less) to the hero's front (180 degrees). Each shot is a separate attack roll, fired at a -2 penalty.

### Lassoes

Sometimes it is better for a cowboy to capture his prey rather than filling it full of lead. On these occasions, lassoes come in quite handy. A lasso is simply a length of rope (typically twenty feet/seven meters or less) with a sliding loop at the end. In day-to-day use, ranch hands hurl them at stray cattle. With a good throw, the loop falls over the animal's head and the cowboy tugs to pull it tight. Then he wraps a loop around the pommel of his saddle and uses his horse to drag the steer back to the herd. In a rodeo or any other time when a steer must to be taken down ("bulldogged"), the cowboy might jump down and wrap the rope tightly around the steer's legs, thereby immobilizing it. This is often done to brand a cow, since the animal is not likely to remain still when scorched with a hot iron.

In the conflict-ridden worlds of *Fistful o' Zombies*, the lasso is more likely used on human prey or for dramatic tricks. Cowboys may take Lasso as a new skill. It should normally be used with Dexterity.

Lassoing an animal is a normal Task with no special modifiers. Cows and steers are not intelligent enough to dodge and weave, so those experienced with lassoes have little trouble catching them in their noose (one Success Level is sufficient). More intelligent creatures, humans included, pit a Simple Dexterity Test against the roper's Lasso and Dexterity Task. Should the target win (regardless of what happens with the roper) or the roper fail, the noose is eluded. Should the roper succeed and the target fail, the lasso attempt succeeds.

Every Turn thereafter, a lassoed character may attempt to wiggle or break free. This is another Resisted Task. The attacker uses a Simple Strength Test or a Strength plus Lasso Skill Task. The victim uses Escapism with either Strength or Dexterity (his choice). If the victim does not have Escapism, a Difficult Strength or Dexterity Test is required. Lassoing the neck actually does damage — 2 x Strength, tripled against living creatures.

The victim breaks free with a Dexterity Test success only if the roper fails. The victim ruins the rope if using Strength and gaining two Success Levels. Should the attacker get two Success Levels more than the victim, he has effectively bound the victim. The target's struggles are ineffective until circumstances change. This usually means the attacker leaves the vicinity, the victim manages to find a knife or other sharp object, and so on.

The Zombie Master may alter these rules to fit bizarre creatures that have additional ways to break free of a lasso.

## Horses

No cowboy in the West would be caught dead without his horse. Food, water, shelter, and other people are scattered far and wide across the frontier, so travelers without mounts face serious challenges just staying alive. Horses were so crucial to life, in fact, that the law in the frontier considered stealing one tantamount to murder. Horse-thieving was a hanging offense in just about every state and territory west of the Mississippi.

The statistics for riding horses can be found in *All Flesh Must Be Eaten* (see p. 141), but a few additional rules should be discussed given their prevalence in the genre.

First, any Task that requires steadiness (such as shooting) is much more difficult when a rider sits atop a moving horse. The Zombie Master should enforce a -2 penalty to most Dexterity-based skills performed from horseback. Even a stationary horse stomps about unevenly. Inflict only a -1 penalty to riders whose horses are relatively motionless.

Horses can be used as cover while riding, though this is frowned on by frontier folk. Cowboys who wish to do so may slide under the neck of the animal, hanging there by one hand and firing with the other. This is a Difficult Riding Task, but subtracts -4 from ranged Task rolls to hit the character. Attack results (after modification) of seven or eight have a 50% (1-5 on D10) chance of hitting the horse instead. Failing the Riding Task means the character falls from his mount. Tumbling from a running horse is dangerous. Assuming the animal was moving at a trot or faster and the falling rider makes a Difficult Dexterity Test, he suffers D6 x 2(6) points of damage. Failing the Dexterity Text increases damage to D8 x 2(8).

In relatively flat terrain and good weather, horses can travel 40 miles (60 km) in an eight-hour day at a brisk walk. Poor weather, such as snow or rain or hilly terrain, halves travel time and distance. In emergencies, horses can be pushed to 60 miles (90 km) a day. This takes twelve hours and exhausts the horse—it must walk the following day (only 20 miles/30 km or so). In extreme cases, horses can be galloped for over 60 miles. The Zombie Master should make a Difficult Constitution Test for each

### Zombie Horse

In some of the settings detailed in this book, the zombie plague is not limited to just the humans. Sometimes, the horses get up from their deathbeds and continue to serve their undead masters as grotesque mockeries of their former lives. Zombie horses can be dangerous, needing meat to survive just as their riders, often trampling the victims to a bloody pulp before chowin' down.

**Strength** 6     **Intelligence** -2

**Dexterity** 3     **Perception** 1

**Constitution** 3     **Willpower** 2

**Dead Points** 15     **Speed** 27

**Endurance Points** n/a     **Essence Pool** 15

**Attack:** Hoof D8(4) x Strength

**Skills:** Brawling 2, Notice 3

**Weak Spot:** Brain (or as the setting dictates)

**Getting Around:** Special

**Strength:** Special

**Senses:** Like the Dead; Scent Tracking

**Sustenance:** Occasional; All Flesh Must Be Eaten

**Intelligence:** Dumb as Dead Wood

**Spreading the Love:** According to Deadworld

**Power:** Varies

animal pushed in this way, rolling once every five miles (7.5 km) after the first 60 (90). Failing any of these rolls means the beast dies of exhaustion.

The Pony Express averaged 80 miles (120 km) and more a day, but did so by stopping at regular intervals to obtain fresh horses.

## Showdowns

Anyone who has watched even a handful of Westerns has seen the classic "showdown." Two gunslingers meet in the middle of Main Street at High Noon. They stare each other down until one goes for his gun. The fastest gun smokes, the slowest lies in its owner's dead hand.

Showdowns in *Fistful o' Zombies* Stories are dramatic affairs. Steely-eyed foes stare at each other for several long moments before they draw their smokewagons and spit lead death. When the smoke clears, only one man remains standing.

There are lots of variations depending on the situation, but for the most part, two gunslingers stand 20 yards (meters) apart and stare each other down until one of them makes a move. Both men then fire and pray. The fastest gun usually wins because of the range and the relative competence of the two parties, but this is not always the case. A slow shot to the brainpan is far better than a fast shot into the photography shop next door.

To begin, the two gunslingers attempt a Resisted Willpower and Intimidation Task. The Zombie Master can allow one such roll, or continue the rolling until one succeeds and the other fails. In that case, the winner adds +2 to his upcoming Initiative roll for the draw. When all the squinting and scowling is done, both fighters roll Initiative. The random system for determining Initiative is always used in showdowns (see *AFMBE*, p. 90). Characters with the Fast Reaction Quality add +2 to this Initiative roll. A character with Fast as Hell adds an additional +3 to the roll. If a hero in the fight decides to let his opponent draw first, he suffers a -3 penalty to his roll. (Good guys in the Singing Cowboys setting, see pp. 44-63, always let their opponents draw first.)

Shots are resolved in order of rolled Initiative. Note that if one character let another draw first (very important if the law is around), then a high Initiative roll means the hero saw his opponent flinch and simply beat him on the draw. It does not necessarily mean he is guilty of firing first.

A single shot does not always end a gunfight at High Noon. On the second or later rounds, both gunslingers roll Initiative and fire normally. Zombie Masters who do not normally allow a roll for Initiative may resume that practice at this point.

## Hanging

Hanging is a common sentence in the West. The victim's hands are tied behind his back and he is dropped from a gallows in the town square. A horse might be driven out from under him or he might be simply hauled up a "hangin' tree." Should a Cast Member ever be the main guest at a necktie party, these quick rules should handle the results.

Most hanging victims are first dropped two to four feet (one meter). This usually breaks their neck and, at least to the hardy folks of the frontier, causes a fast, humane death. In such circumstances, the character must succeed at a Survival Test with a -1 penalty. The Zombie Master may inflict a -3 penalty for a long drop (five-six feet/two meters or more). Failure results in death. Success merely avoids instant death.

Should an hombre suffer a long drop, there is a significant risk his head pops off. Use the Rule of 1 here. If the Survival Test result is a one, roll again. On a second roll of five or less, the victim's head is grotesquely pulled from his twitching corpse.

Assuming the character lives through the initial drop, he quickly begins to suffocate as the weight of his own body pulls against the rope around his throat. The victim suffers D4 points of damage per Turn from this point until he is dead.

# Guns of the West

Guns in the old days were not as precisely manufactured or as easy to use as they are in modern day. The following tables cover most weapons used in the West. The Weapons Tables cover range, damage, and EV. The Availability Tables provide Cap, Cost, Date (when the weapon was first available), and Aval for specific weapons of a given type. Descriptions follow the tables.

## Ranged Weapons Table

| Weapon | Range | Damage | EV |
|---|---|---|---|
| SB Pistols/Derringers | 1/3/5/10/30 | D8 x 2(8)* | 2/1 |
| Pistols | 3/10/20/40/75 | D8 x 3(12)* | 1/1 |
| SB Muskets | 5/10/20/50/100 | D8 x 4(16)* | 10/5 |
| Rifled Muskets | 10/25/75/150/300 | D8 x 5(20)* | 10/5 |
| Carbine | 5/10/25/75/150 | D8 x 4(16)* | 1/1 |
| Rifles | 10/25/75/150/300 | D8 x 5(20)* | 8/4 |
| Shotgun (Buckshot only) | 10/30/50/100/200 | D8 x 6(24)# | 8/4 |
| Napoleon Cannon | 50/100/300/700/1500 | D10 x 10(50) | n/a |
| Gatling Gun (.58) | 10/25/75/150/300 | D8 x 5(20)* | 20/10 |
| Bow and Arrow | 3/10/20/40/75 | D6 x 2(12)@ | 2/1 (per 20) |
| Tomahawk | 3/5/8/10/13 | (D4 + 1)(3) x Strength@ | 1/1 |

## Close Combat Weapons Table

| Weapon Type | Damage | EV |
|---|---|---|
| Tomahawk | D6(3) x Strength@ | 1/1 |
| War Lance | D6(3) x Strength@ | 4/2 |
| Saber | D8(4) x Strength@ | 2/1 |

* Use normal bullet damage (see *AFMBE*, p. 105).

# Use shot damage (see *AFMBE*, p. 105).

@ Use slashing/stabbing damage (see *AFMBE*, p. 105).

## Weapons Availability Table

| Weapon | Cap | Cost | Date | Aval |
|---|---|---|---|---|
| SB Percussion Pistols and Derringers | 1 | $10 | 1800+ | C |
| Derringer | 2 | $5 | 1825 | U |
| Colt Walker Pistol (.44) | 6 | $20 | 1847 | C |
| Colt Dragoon Pistol (.44) | 6 | $18 | 1848 | C |
| LeMat Pistol (.42) | 9 | $25 | 1856 | R |
| Volcanic Pistol (.41) | 10 | $15 | 1857 | R |
| Colt Peacemaker Pistol (.45) | 6 | $10 | 1873 | C |
| Colt Lightning Pistol (.38) | 6 | $15 | 1877 | C |
| S&W Frontier Pistol (.44-40) | 6 | $15 | 1880 | C |
| | | | | |
| SB Percussion Muskets | 1 | $10 | 1800+ | C |
| Kentucky Rifle | 1 | $15 | 1800+ | C |
| Rifled Muskets | 1 | $20 | 1855+ | C |
| | | | | |
| Sharps Carbine (.52) | 1 | $10 | 1851 | U |
| Spencer Carbine (.56) | 7 | $20 | 1851 | U |
| Springfield Carbine (.45-.70) | 1 | $10 | 1870 | U |
| | | | | |
| Sharps Rifle (.52) | 1 | $15 | 1851 | U |
| Henry Repeater Rifle (.44) | 15 | $42 | 1862 | U |
| Winchester '73 Rifle (.44-40) | 15 | $25 | 1873 | C |
| Winchester '76 Rifle (.45-.70) | 15 | $25 | 1873 | C |
| Sharps Big Rifle (.50) | 1 | $20 | 1875 | U |
| | | | | |
| Double Barrel Shotgun | 2 | $10 | 1836+ | C |
| Revolving Shotgun | 6 | $25 | 1839 | R |
| | | | | |
| Napoleon Cannon | 1 | $1000 | 1800+ | R |
| Gatling Gun (.58) | 100 | $150 | 1862 | R |
| | | | | |
| Bow and Arrow | n/a | $10 | All | C |
| Tomahawk | n/a | $5 | All | U |
| War Lance | n/a | $50 | All | U |
| Saber | n/a | $20 | All | U |

# Weapon Descriptions

**Bow and Arrow:** Indian bows were not nearly as strong as English longbows, so players used to the long ranges of fantasy games should be warned. Historical accounts often detail soldiers surviving hits by literally dozens of arrows. Only an arrow that punctured a major organ, vein or artery would kill in a hurry. Lesser hits might cause a subject to bleed to death soon after, but instant death was quite rare. Arrows are fairly expensive to buy (20 for $1) as they are not commonly available for purchase. Cast Members who wish to make their own arrows can do so by spending a few hours scavenging a wooded area and making a Dexterity and Craft (Fletching) Task roll.

**Derringer:** The original was made by Henry Deringer—knockoffs were later known as "Derringers." Note the different spelling for those guns made by those other than Henry Deringer. All Derringers come in many calibers, but .41 was most popular. These tiny guns are easily concealed—subtract two from the roll of anyone attempting to perceive a Derringer or other "holdout" pistol.

**Dynamite:** Early dynamite is simply sawdust soaked in nitro. The area of effect is 3/10/20, and damage is D6 x 2(6) times the number of sticks. This damage is doubled at Ground Zero, normal in the General Effect zone and halved up to the Maximum Range.

**Gatling Gun:** Gatlings quickly became the terrors of the battlefield as the Plains Indians Wars began. This gun can only be used in two ways: Rock n' Roll and Automatic Fire (see *AFMBE*, pp. 102-103). Gatlings are mounted on tripods—they cannot be carried around Rambo-style. Some are even mounted on carriages for use in mobile warfare. Custer had such a weapon, but chose to leave it behind when advancing on the Little Bighorn.

**Kentucky Rifle:** Early muskets are traditionally unrifled, making them very inaccurate, but faster to load than rifles which require more time to ram the round down the barrel. In an Old West setting, the differences are very important—a character must choose between the increased accuracy of a rifled gun versus the faster loading speed of a smoothbore musket. The Kentucky Rifle is reloaded like the Smoothbore Percussion Musket, but with base reload time of eight Turns instead of five. Additional Success Levels when reloading can lower this to a minimum of three Turns.

**LeMat Pistol:** This curious nine-shot revolver also has a small shotgun attached under its barrel. Treat the range on the secondary weapon as if it were a Derringer, but with the damage of a shotgun. The shotgun holds a single shell.

**Napoleon Cannon:** Cowpokes who really need to make something dead can always try a smoothbore cannon. The most popular gun of the time fires a 12-pound metal shell. Unless the shot hits a solid object, like stone or a tree, it continues on through the target and into any other targets in its path. Each hit after the first reduces its damage by one multiple (D10 x 9(45), D10 x 8(40), and so on). Other ammunition is also available for blasting apart hordes of groaning undead. Shrapnel shells detonate with a blast radius of 3/8/15 for D6 x 8(24), D6 x 5(15) and D6 x 3(9) damage, respectively. Canister is a hailstorm of small balls much like a giant shotgun. It is only effective up to about 100 yards (short range). Anyone in the arc of fire is hit by D6 balls, each one causing D6 x 3(9) damage. Prone troops have a 50% (1-5 on D10) chance of being missed altogether. The average cannon weighs in the area of 1,500 pounds (750 kg), so horses or a bunch of men are required to move this baby.

**Nitroglycerine:** Nitro brings a whole new level of fun to blowing up zombies. This delicate liquid explodes if shaken roughly or exposed to heat or flame. The burst radius is 1/5/10. The base damage is D10(5) and each ounce increases the multiplier by one. Damage is doubled at Ground Zero, normal at the General Effect range, and halved at Maximum Range.

**Rifled Musket:** Loading a rifled gun was a very slow process prior to the invention of the Minié ball by Claude-Étienne Minié. This ingenious bullet was small enough to ram down the barrel, but expanded on firing to better fit the barrel's rifling. The round itself is simply a cylindrical bullet with a conical point and an iron cup in the hollow base. When fired, the force pushes upward on the cup, expanding the metal so that it fits snugly against the rifling.

From this point on the Kentucky Rifle and similar weapons were no longer significantly better than rifled "Minié" muskets. These muskets use the same reloading rules as the SB Percussion Muskets, but with a greater range.

**SB Percussion Pistol:** These smoothbore weapons are good for an opening volley, but are most useful as clubs afterwards due to their slow reloading times. Packing a new bullet in such a pistol is a Dexterity and Guns (Musket) Task that requires two Turns. Rolling two Success Levels or better reduces the amount of time required to one Turn. On an unmodified roll of one, or if the Guns Task total is less than five, the user misses a step and must begin again.

**SB Percussion Musket:** These heavy smoothbore weapons were the main armament of the world for several hundred years. By the time of the "West," these are percussion-type weapons, meaning the hammer of the weapon falls onto a primer, which detonates the powder in a cartridge and propels the shell down an unrifled, and thus inaccurate, barrel. Reloading a "black powder" weapon is a lengthy process. The firer must place a paper cartridge and metal ball (the bullet, often called a "round") down the barrel using a ramrod and replace the ramrod in its sleeve (under the barrel). Then he must cock the weapon, aim and fire. This takes considerable time — five Turns with a successful Dexterity and Guns (Musket) Task roll. Every additional Success Level reduces the number of Turns needed to reload by one to a minimum of two Turns (around 10 seconds — an incredibly fast reload). Unfortunately, these guns are subject to frequent misfires due to human error. On an unmodified roll of one, or if the loading Guns Task total is less than five, the firer has forgotten some crucial step in the reloading process. The gun misfires and must be reloaded. Add an additional D4(2) Turns of work to account for cleaning up the previous mess.

**Sharps Big .50 Rifle:** This weapon was designed to kill buffaloes and fires a massive .50 caliber round.

**Tomahawk:** The traditional axe of the Indians becomes rare by 1870 or so, but a few were used even at the Little Bighorn in 1876. These light weapons may be thrown as well as used in hand-to-hand combat.

**Volcanic Pistol:** This odd weapon featured Hunt "rocket balls," so named because the slug contained the powder. These early repeaters were not very reliable. Using the Rule of 1, a negative result number means the gun is jammed, requiring D6 x 2(6) minutes to repair.

**War Lance:** The Plains Indians used these long, light spears early in their clashes with white men, but quickly phased them out as firearms became available. The lance damage uses the rider's or the mounts Strength, whichever is higher. Double the damage if the wielder and mount are able to charge at least ten yards (meters) before striking the opponent. The lance sticks in any character who takes more than ten points of damage from a mounted strike. Pulling it out costs the impaled D6 x 2(6) Life Points unless an Intelligence and Medicine (Surgery) Task is made. While impaled, a character suffers a -2 penalty to any tasks that require mobility and loses one-quarter of his normal movement. Heavy running or riding causes blood loss at the rate of one Life Point per Turn spent in such activity.

# Money

The following table describes common currencies and their names in the West.

| | |
|---|---|
| $20 | Double Eagle |
| $10 | Gold Eagle |
| $5 | Half Eagle |
| $2.50 | Quarter Eagle |
| $1 | Silver Dollar |
| $.50 | Half Dollar |
| $.25 | Quarter Dollar |
| $.10 | Dime |
| $.05 | Half Dime (later, nickel) |
| $.02 | Two Cent Piece |
| $.01 | Cent |
| $.005 | Half Cent |

# Equipment

The following equipment and services are available in this era at the prices listed.

## Ammunition

| | |
|---|---|
| Percussion Caps | $.50/100 |
| Pistol Ammo | $4/100 |
| Rifle Ammo | $5/100 |
| Arrow | $1/20 |

## Goods

| | |
|---|---|
| Axe | $2 |
| Barbed Wire | $1/50 yards |
| Bible | $5 |
| Binoculars (1848+) | $15 |
| Boots | $8 |
| Candles (1 doz.) | $.25 |
| Card Deck | $.25 |
| Chaps | $5 |
| Cigar | $.05 |
| Dime Novel | $.10 |
| Dress | $2 |
| Dynamite | $1/stick |
| Hammer | $1 |
| Hat (most styles) | $5 |
| Hat (Stetson) | $25 |
| Holster | $2 |
| Holster, swivel | $5 |
| Knife, pocket | $.50 |
| Lantern | $1 |
| Matches, safety | $.75 |
| Newspaper | $.50 |
| Nitroglycerine (1847) | $.50 |
| Pick | $1 |
| Pocket watch | $5 |
| Rope | $.10/yard |

| | |
|---|---|
| Saw | $1 |
| Shirt | $.50 |
| Shoes | $4 |
| Shovel | $.50 |
| Soap | $.05 |
| Spurs | $2 |
| Stable | $.25 |
| Suit | $10 |
| Tobacco | $.10/oz |
| Trousers | $1 |
| Trunk | $8 |
| Winter Coat | $10 |

## Boarding and Food

| | |
|---|---|
| Bath | $.50 |
| Beer, glass | $.05 |
| Brothel | $5/night |
| Coffee | $.25/lb |
| Flour | $3/50lb sack |
| Hotel, average | $1/night |
| Hotel, upscale | $5/night |
| Meal, average | $.25 |
| Meal, good | $1+ |
| Tea | $.10/12 oz. |
| Whiskey, shot | $.10 |
| Whiskey, bottle | $1+ |

## Travel Fares

| | |
|---|---|
| Riverboat | $5/day |
| Stagecoach | $3/50 miles |
| Train, 2nd class | $.05/mile |
| Train, 1st class | $.10/mile |

## Animals

| | |
|---|---|
| Horse | $100 |
| Mule | $5 |

# Bandita
## Norm

**Str** 3 **Dex** 3 **Con** 2
**Int** 2 **Per** 3 **Wil** 2
**LPs** 30
**EPs** 26
**Spd** 10
**Essence** 15

## Qualities/Drawbacks

Addiction (Alcohol) (-1)
Addiction (Smokes) (-2)
Cruel (-1)
Minority (Mexican) (-2)
Nerves of Steel (3)
Paranoid (-2)
Secret (Wanted in various territories) (-2)
Situational Awareness (2)

## Skills

Brawling 3
Cheating 2
Demolitions 2
Escapism 2
Gambling 2
Guns (Handgun) 3
Guns (Rifle) 3
Guns (Shotgun) 2
Hand Weapon (Knife) 3
Intimidation 3
Language (English) 2
Notice 3
Riding (Horse) 3
Survival (Desert) 3
Survival (Mountains) 2

## Gear

Colt Dragoon with 24 Shots, Colt Walker with 12
Shots, Double Barrel Shotgun with 6 Shots,
Dynamite (5 sticks), Really, Really Big Knife (does
short sword damage), Bottle of Tequila,
Plenty of Tobacco, Stick Matches

## Personality

Are you looking at me?

No me mires, chivato. I don't like it when gringos stare at me. Last time a gringo looked at me, I shot him.

And when the dead cabrón got back up, I shot him again. Así es.

So, if you think I might be getting flojo because a few dead pendejos came out of their graves in Tijuana, you're wrong. Everyone who rides with me knows I'll rob you then kill you twice and take the gold from your teeth. You better look the other way, gabacho, or I'll make sure you never see again.

## Quote

You shouldn't have recognized me, chivato. Now I'll kill you—as many times as it takes.

# Cowboy
## Norm

**Str** 3 **Dex** 3 **Con** 3
**Int** 2 **Per** 2 **Wil** 2
**LPs** 40
**EPs** 29
**Spd** 12
**Essence** 15

## Qualities/Drawbacks
Addiction (Drinking) (-1)
Fast Reaction Time (2)
Hard to Kill 2 (2)
Reckless or Showoff (-2)
Resistance
(Disease) 2 (2)

## Skills
Brawling 3
Gambling 2
Guns (Handgun) 3
Guns (Rifle) 2
Hand Weapon (Knife) 2
Lasso 4
Notice 2
Riding (Horse) 4
Survival (Prairie) 3
Survival (Desert) 3
Tracking 2

## Gear
Colt Walker with 12 Shots,
Sharps Rifle, Henry Repeater or
Winchester '73 with 30 Shots,
Knife, Horse, Saddle, Canteen,
Tin Cup, Lasso, Matches,
Saddlebag, Sleeping Roll

## Personality
Slide on over pardner, give a guy some room.
BARTENDER!!! Whiskey for me and somethin' for
the tenderfoot here.

Ya won't believe this.
There I was, ridin'
herd on some of Ol'
Smitty's steer, when out
yonder way I hear this hella-
cious noise. So I kick ol' Bessie
into a slow jog over the rise and
see what looks to be a squatter
tryin' ta rustle himself a li'l dogie,
and I thinks we got ourselfs cause
for a li'l necktie social.

Turns out ta be Miss Pammy
from Rosie's Saloon . . . yup . . .
the one who got herself kilt in that shootout
las' week. There she was . . . lookin'
deader'n hell . . . and chewin' on that
calf!!!

And if that don't beat all . . . she
turned and tried to eat mah horse!!!

So's I did what any god-fearin'
man woulda done. I blew the
wench's head off.

## Quote
"What in tarna-
tion!?!?! Dammit ya
varmint . . . quit tryin' ta
chew on mah horse!!!"
<BLAM!!> <BLAM!!>
<BLAM!!>

# Gambler
## Norm

**Str** 2 **Dex** 3 **Con** 2
**Int** 2 **Per** 4 **Wil** 3
**LPs** 26
**EPs** 26
**Spd** 10
**Essence** 17

## Qualities/Drawbacks

Covetous (Greedy) 2 (-2)
Fast Reaction Time (2)
Obsession (Gambling) (-2)
Good Luck 3 (3)

## Skills

Brawling 2
Cheating 4
Dodge 2
Gambling 4
Guns (Handgun) 2
Hand Weapon (Club) 2
Notice 3
Riding (Horses) 2
Sleight of Hand 4
Smooth Talking 3
Streetwise 2

## Gear

Colt Walker with 12 Shots, 4-shot
Pepperbox Derringer with 12 Rounds
(up sleeve), Fancy Walking Stick
(doubles as a club), Lucky Deck
of Cards, $50.00 in Winnings

## Personality

I was in Laramie, at Billy's Saloon, playing Faro.
Stinky Johnson, one of the local miners,
walked in. He always had a faraway look—
but that day his eyes were different.

He walked to the bar, where Billy was
already pouring his drink. Stinky paused
for a few seconds . . . and then bit Billy's
hand. He stood there with a chunk of
flesh hanging from his mouth, gnawing
slowly.

I gathered my winnings and made my
way to the door. I knew when to fold
. . . and when to run. As I was leaving, Billy put several slugs into him,
but Stinky didn't noticed. After that, I
didn't stick around.

Those eyes—I'll never get that look out
of my mind.

## Quote

"My Colt beats the aces up your
sleeve."

# Saloon Girl
## Norm

Str 1  Dex 4  Con 3
Int 2  Per 3  Wil 3
LPs 26
EPs 26
Spd 14
Essence 16

## Qualities/Drawbacks

Addiction (Drinking) (-1)
Attractiveness +2 (2)
Charisma +2 (2)
Covetous (Greedy) 2 (-2)
Resistance (Pain) 2 (2)
Showoff (-2)

## Skills

Beautician 2
Cheating 3
Dancing 2
Dodge 2
Gambling 2
Guns (Handgun) 2
Haggling 3
Hand Weapon (Knife) 3
Notice 3
Pick Pocket 3
Seduction 3
Smooth Talking 3

## Gear

Knife with Thigh Sheath, Makeup Kit and Mirror, Various Clothes, Shoes

## Personality

We came out West with great hopes. Jack bought some land that should have made us rich. Unfortunately, the land wasn't quite so great, but it didn't really matter because it turned out the land didn't really belong to us after all. We were stuck here with no land and not much money. It took only a week for Jack to drink what money we had left and get killed in a bar fight.

That left me without a penny to my name. I did manage to get a job in the local saloon, but they "expected" certain things from a gal with a figure like mine. Didn't have much choice really. I learned two things working in the saloon. The first was Jack was not the only male fool in the world; men and foolishness seemed to go hand in hand. The second thing was that a girl could make twice the amount from "horizontal singing" that she could from farming. I've heard stories from some of the girls, but nothing bad has happened to me yet.

So I get by. I always do. Still, there has got to be something better for me out there.

## Quote

"I can do that for you darling, but it's going to cost you."

# CHAPTER THREE

# SINGING COWBOYS

# Rex

Manly put away his guitar and saddled up Dusty the Wonder Horse. It was morning and the sun rose high in the east. Rex downed the last of his coffee, shoved the guitar into his custom-made saddle holster, then mounted—Dusty knelt down for him without command.

The town of Carter's Creek was just another dustpan somewhere in the wide-open spaces of the West. Rex had seen a hundred of these towns. Every one of them thought they were different, but they were really all the same. Sure, the names varied, and you never knew if the cattle king, railroad baron, or sheep farmers were the bad guys, but it was always one of those three.

They all had a town drunk as well. He was always a friendly fellow who often happened to overhear the bad guys' plans—he'd usually reveal them to Rex just before the showdown with the hired gun they brought in to take him out.

There was always a beautiful girl, too. Sometimes she was the Mayor's daughter. Sometimes she was the Sheriff's or the sheep farmer's daughter. Her mother was always dead and she was something of a free-spirited Tomboy. Rex had sung to many of these and had even received a reckless peck on the cheek from a few for saving the day.

There was usually another woman in these towns as well, working at the local saloon. She was older, more exotic; a dark and dangerous beauty, often Mexican. Her name was Kitty, Kelly, or Esmeralda. Though Rex was sure she was a "soiled dove," she never actually "worked." In fact, Rex had never met a man who had truthfully been with her. "Esmeralda" had bewitching eyes but a heart of gold. She also had a thing for Rex, and if properly played, was another great source of warning should the town drunk fall through.

The cattle kings and rail barons were most often the bad guys. The cattle kings loved barbed wire and didn't seem to care if the sheep farmer's stock got all tangled up in it. (Rex never thought about what a mess that must make and he certainly never saw it.) In the seventy-three towns he had "cleaned up," Rex had only found the sheep farmers to be the bad guys once. That one had thrown him for a bit.

Their minions were the goons—a passel of cheap toughs who thought they ruled the frontier. Rex chuckled when he thought of how many guns he had shot out of their hands. The surprise and shock usually chased them away. If it didn't, it was time for fisticuffs. Rex excelled at fighting and though he told the children that violence never solved anything, his knuckles bore the calluses of the lessons he'd taught the black hats.

Once the goons had been trounced, the cattle king or rail baron got nasty. That's when a gunslinger with a moniker like "Black Bart" or "Black River Steve" arrived on the morning train or stage. "Blood Creek" Kane had been one of the toughest fights. He wore a white hat, and for a short time, Rex wasn't sure if he was really a bad guy. Turned out it was just a trick (sometimes the bad guys were clever like that), but Rex had shot the guns right out of Kane's hands, kicked him in the backside and sent him Back East on the 12:01 stage.

Yup, Rex thought. All these towns were just the same. Town drunks, saloon gals, cattle kings, rail barons, sheep farmers, and gunmen.

Oh . . . . and zombies.

# Singing Cowboys

Gene Autry, Roy Rogers, and Dale Evans made a slew of Westerns in the early 1930s and 1940s. Millions of viewers flocked to theatres to watch the "singing cowboys" fight the bad guys week after week. Most of their adventures took place in "serials," short episodes ending in cliffhangers to keep audiences coming back to see what happened next week. After solving the mystery and rounding up the bad guys, the good guys often did what all cowboys of the Old West did. They sang.

Okay, maybe it didn't really happen like that, but in this genre, the world is a better place. Things are simpler and characters are drawn in clear black and white. Good guys wear white hats and rhinestone suits; bad guys obligingly wear black. The good guys have names like Rex, Tom, Roy, or Gene. Bad guys have nicknames like "Seven Shot" Moran, "Two-Gun" Martin or "Trick-Shot" Kelly. Good guys name their horses as well—Comet, Trigger, Silver, or Dusty. Bad guys do not care about their horses. Heroes keep faithful gals like Dale, Lois, or Becky around, even though they get kidnapped and tied to railroad tracks a lot. Bad guys never have girlfriends. White hats have friends like Gabby or Tonto. They get kidnapped and tied to railroad tracks a lot too, but when the hero gets cornered, these sidekicks always show up in the nick of time. Black hats travel in large groups that look like friends, but they really do not care much for each other. They do not even help each other much in a fight—that is why they usually attack the good guys one at a time.

Finally, one hit from a hero's fist is enough to knock most thugs out cold. If the villain is armed, a quick shot to the gun levels the playing field. The bad guys shoot people (when they manage to hit), but blood or gore just do not happen.

This is the era of the Singing Cowboys.

With zombies.

> This here is a even chapter and should use "she/her" as the generic reference, but that's just silly for this Deadworld. Singing Cowboys bad guys are always male (though a female bad guy would be a nice twist) and we will refer to them that way.

# Start Singin'

The tales of the Singing Cowboys are not based in reality. These adventures come from Hollywood hijinks and the simple, good-natured era of the 1930s. That means heroes do not shoot villains when they can avoid it—they shoot the guns out of their hands instead. And the white hats do not die on the odd occasion a villain gets the drop on them. They might be injured or more likely "knocked out" for a while, but they always come back in top form for the final showdown.

For the most part, the Cast Members participate in adventures right out of the Saturday morning serials—with the unusual addition of a few walking dead.

## Mandatory Skills, Qualities and Drawbacks

All Cast Members except Sidekicks (see below) must have the following:

**Qualities**
Balladeer
Hard to Kill 3 or better

**Drawbacks**
Honorable 3
Law of the West

**Skills**
Singing 1 or higher
Guns 3 or higher
Riding 3 or higher

## New Qualities and Drawbacks

### Balladeer
#### 1-point Physical Quality

Singing Cowboys, to put it bluntly, sing. That is why every hero in this setting has the Balladeer Quality and must have a Singing skill at level 1 or better. Heroes with golden voices (high Singing Skills) can perform near magical feats.

**Songs:** A cowboy who sings a song has a miraculous and inspiring effect on her companions. The kinds of songs that can be sung are listed below. To complete a song, the player simply makes a Constitution and Singing Task. If successful, the song has its effect. If the song fails, it has no effect. Regardless of success or failure, no cowboy in the group may try that song again this game session. Also, only two songs may be sung during any game session. Players should choose carefully and sing only after they have encountered the villains and know what kind of help they may need.

A Singing Cowboy may sing a song to trigger one of the effects below. Each attempt requires about five minutes of quiet time—usually around a campfire. These are not songs a hero can sing during a raging gunfight or barroom brawl.

If the *player* actually sings a short tune, she gets to add +3 to the roll. Others in the group are welcome to join in.

**Courage:** Ballads of brave deeds and noble sacrifices are sung when the hero's team has suffered a setback but must move on to defeat the Story's villain. Every white hat in the party adds +4 to her next Willpower Test if the Singing Task is made.

**Fortitude:** A ballad about toughing it out under the harshest conditions may inspire the good guys to keep going even when they have suffered personal injury. The heroes gain D10 Life Points (roll individually) for the duration of the session, but the song may only be sung after someone in the party has suffered at least minor damage in a previous scene.

**Inspiration:** The best songs are those that inspire the team to great deeds. Each hero may reroll any Test or Task made during the game session when this song is sung. This is a great song to open the game with. Perhaps the group even has a particular "theme" song for their gang. If the theme song is established over two or more sessions, the Zombie Master may allow this song to be sung for free and not count against the usual two-song limit. Of course, the players must actually sing their theme song at the beginning of the session to gain this award and all must join in.

**Soothing:** The cowboy puts any locals who can hear the song at ease. This can disburse a lynch mob, calm a town plagued by zombies, stay the hand of an over-excited hero, or perhaps even convince a number of locals to join the heroes in their fight against the black hats.

**Speed:** All the heroes gain +2 to their Initiative rolls in the next combat that occurs this play session. If the Zombie Master does not use the random Initiative system, the bonus applies to any and all heroes who take part in a showdown this session. The song is usually about a gunfight at High Noon and concerns the hero keeping her cool while the villain tries to draw too fast and fumbles her shot.

**Ballad:** This song can only be sung when a white hat is slain. The singing *Cast Member* must make a Very Difficult (-4) Singing Task roll, and the *player* must actually concoct a short song as well. If the roll is made, every true member of the party (not extras, hirelings and hangers-on) feels a little piece of the fallen hero's soul flow into her. However many experience points the character would have gained for the night are added to each of her companions' session totals. If this is a one-shot where experience points are of no consequence, the Cast Members get a reroll as described under "Inspiration" above. Of course, the hero must say something appropriate when she uses the reroll, such as "This one's for Rex!"

With six Success Levels, the Zombie Master may actually have the character miraculously return to life. Maybe everyone saw her fall in the old mine shaft covered in zombies, but she somehow survived and now comes limping back into the camp with only a few scratches. This one is entirely up to the Zombie Master, the circumstances of the character's "death," and most importantly, the song sung by her lonesome compadres.

## Law of the West
### 5-point Mental Drawback

The Law of the West is a mantra for every hero in this genre. The heroes live and die by a strict code that defines what makes a man or woman good and true. As such, it is mandatory for every Cast Member except a Sidekick.

> ## The Law of the West, as written by Gene Autry himself.
>
> A cowboy . . .
>
> "... must not take unfair advantage of an enemy."
>
> "... must never go back on his word."
>
> "... must always tell the truth."
>
> "... must always be gentle with children, elderly people, and animals."
>
> "... must not possess racially or religious intolerant ideas."
>
> "... must help people in distress."
>
> "... must be a good worker."
>
> "... must respect women, parents, and his nation's laws."
>
> "... must neither drink or smoke."
>
> "... must be a patriot."

Heroes must follow these rules very strictly. Singing Cowboys who break the Law of the West face rough times indeed. When such a heinous event occurs, a chain of events begins immediately. First off, if there is any possible way for folks to know what has happened, they do. Everyone from the town drunk ("I can't believe you lied to Widow McGillicutty—what a sorry day this is, Rex") to the cowboy's companions instantly knows she has violated the sacred oath. Second, the hero loses experience points that would otherwise have been awarded at the end of the session. The exact amount depends on the violation. A white lie or taking a drink at the local saloon costs the hero one point. Getting in a drunken brawl at a brothel costs everything, including the hero's reputation. Some crimes have far more consequences than just the loss of experience. Should a hero ever do something truly heinous, like gunning down a lawman in the course of betraying her country for a bushel of peyote, she loses her "good gal" status altogether and every white hat in the country shows up on the next train to shoot the guns out of her hands and throw her in the "hoosegow" forever.

On the flip side, heroes who really put themselves out to follow the Law of the West should get extra experience points at the end of the session. This is entirely up to the Zombie Master and her perception of how much trouble obeying this strict code caused the hero and her companions.

The Law of the West might work as follows in a typical adventure. Say a band of Singing Cowboys decides to infiltrate a gang of masked bandits to find out who their mysterious leader is. They could put on masks and pretend to be one of the bad guys, but they could not drink or smoke with the gang while waiting for the next holdup. When the bandits announced their plans, the Cast Members would have to find a way to sabotage them. And when they finally cornered the leader, they would have to reveal themselves before drawing their guns. It just would not be honorable any other way.

## Sidekick

### 1- to 5-point Social Quality

If the Zombie Master allows it, one Cast Member (and only one) may have Sidekick as a Quality. Sidekicks are incredibly loyal minor heroes that accompany the Singing Cowboy on her many adventures. They are not meant simply to be an extra gun or to soak up bullets for the hero—they are more of a plot device, comic relief, and foil for the Zombie Master. Sidekicks are especially appropriate if the group is small. The player with the Sidekick can ask or even order her companion around as appropriate, but the companion should always be played by the Zombie Master. Though loyal, a sidekick does have a mind of her own.

Sidekicks are Norms, and have fifteen points for Attributes, five for Qualities, and thirty for skills. They may take up to ten points in Drawbacks. Sidekicks are not as perfect as the heroes and so may have mild addictions to alcohol or tobacco (for one point). They may also take a one-point Drawback in Covetous or Cowardly, or a two-point Drawback in Lazy—all Drawbacks normally forbidden to heroes in this genre. The Sidekick must be completely loyal to a Singing Cowboy Cast Member. She follows orders and gives her life for the "boss" if necessary. Of course, the boss does the same for her as well.

Sidekicks are often as much trouble as they are help. They always have a tragic flaw of some sort that causes trouble at the most inopportune moment. Usually, the trouble is caused by simple gross incompetence or mild alcoholism. Sometimes, however, Sidekicks are simply a minority and the bigotry and ignorance of others are the source of their problems. Tonto could not enter some saloons, for instance, and so could not perform certain tasks for his companion the Lone Ranger.

## Sidekicks as Cast Members

If the Zombie Master allows it, a character may declare himself a "Sidekick." She should make her character using the rules for Sidekicks as written.

Playing a Sidekick can be quite a role-playing challenge. The character is not as tough or as glamorous as a Singing Cowboy, but is tremendously fun in other ways. The Cowboy's girlfriend might be able to take the Sidekick in a fair fight, but the challenge and the fun of playing Tonto or "Gabby" Hayes can be worth far more than being able to shoot the guns out of the bad guys' hands. The Zombie Master should suitably reward a player who is willing to take a back seat for the good of the party or adventure.

## Wonder Horse
**Strength** 6 | **Intelligence** 2
**Dexterity** 5 | **Perception** 4
**Constitution** 5 | **Willpower** 5
**Life Points** 65 | **Speed** 33
**Endurance Points:** n/a | **Essence Pool:** 27
**Attack:** Hoof D8(4) x 6
**Skills:** Brawling 4, Notice 3

## Wonder Horse
### 3-point Social Quality

A Wonder Horse is a stout and intelligent beast with a name like Trigger, Stardust, or Champion, who has an uncanny knack of saving the hero's bacon at times. The horse is eerily intelligent, but also stubborn, feisty, and perhaps even a bit bloodthirsty when it comes to biting at bad guys (including zombies). They are terrified of zombies the first time they meet them, but quickly develop a hatred for these unnatural creatures after a single encounter. Wonder Horses do not hesitate to charge in and bite, stomp, and kick the living dead after their first encounter.

Wonder Horses can understand any simple commands their owners give them, and can even "talk" back as well. Understanding the whinnies and hoof-stomps of a character's Wonder Horse requires a Simple Intelligence Test. Complex messages require a Difficult Test. Trying to communicate that Jane is being held in the old mine is difficult, but getting the hero to mount up and ride there is very simple.

## Recommended Qualities and Drawbacks

Some particularly appropriate Qualities and Drawbacks are Adversary, Attractiveness, Charisma, Hard to Kill, Honorable, Nerves Of Steel, Reckless, Resistance, Secret (such as the Lone Ranger's secret identity), and Showoff.

## Restricted Qualities and Drawbacks

Because of the Law of the West (see p. 49), heroes may never have any of the following Drawbacks: Addiction, Covetous, Cowardly, Cruel, or Lazy.

# Combat Rules

The Singing Cowboys Deadworld requires a few additional rules to properly manage the flavor of the genre. Most of these pertain to combat and the odd way in which most fights are decidedly non-lethal.

**Cover:** For some odd reason, rocks, crates piled around rail stations, water troughs, and other forms of cover make both black and white hats nearly impossible to hit, even though neither side makes the best use of it. For this reason, characters who duck and cover (see *AFMBE*, p. 101) in a Singing Cowboys game may still fire their own weapons, but at a -4 penalty.

**Death:** True heroes are hard to kill. Under most circumstances, a white hat reduced to zero Life Points goes unconscious and does not die (but there are exceptions—see below). The hero then comes around in (D10 x 2) hours with all her Life Points back. If she was in a precarious position when she lost her last Life Points (battling on a rope bridge, hanging from a cliff ledge, in a collapsing mine, and so on), she somehow manages to survive. Maybe she falls into a river far below, stumbles into cover just before passing out or is captured and placed in a death trap instead of slain. The actual events are for the Zombie Master to decide, but do not be surprised if a white hat goes straight from the frying pan into the fire.

Extras, unfortunately, do not get these breaks. Should the pretty saloon gal catch a bullet and lose all her Life Points, a poignant but unavoidable death scene in the hero's tender arms is assured. She very likely passes on some crucial information before passing on, however.

**Death and Zombies:** White hats are not so impervious when the walking dead are involved. Zombies get to break the rules. When shambling dead take down a white hat, she meets the same fate heroes in all other genres face: a one-course Tex-Mex meatfest. Other supernatural varmints encountered get the same break as well. If the Zombie Master throws a werewolf into an adventure, bet that it can kill a white hat dead.

**Indians:** Good guys do not like to fight Indians. They know the red men have gotten a pretty raw deal from the palefaces and try to cut them a little slack. If white hats are confronted by a few Indians, both sides close to fight with fisticuffs. Indians can use tomahawks, knives, or whatever hand weapons they want. Heroes are restricted to fists or pistol and rifle butts. Neither side uses ranged weapons on each other if they can help it—that would not be sporting.

If ten or more Indians are chasing a hero, she may fire her weapon at them. Even then, she does not fire at any individual—she simply fires blindly at the crowd. When a target is downed, he falls from his horse (if mounted) and lies motionless (but surely not dead). The wounded brave always gets up and runs away (nursing his leg, arm or shoulder) at the end of the scene. Rarely—and only as a plot device—an Indian brave may be killed in this way. When this happens, the brave is almost certainly the Chief's son or some other important member of the tribe, starting a semi-violent war between the Indians and the local whites.

Should the Indians win a fight, the good guys are captured and taken before the Chief. The Chief, who speaks perfect, if broken, English, allows the white hats to go free if they prove their innocence through a trial of some sort. This might be as simple as walking barefoot across a bed of coals or as complex as asking for help in getting justice from a crooked trader. It might also involve singing a song so beautiful the Chief's daughter weeps or it may be a simple trial by combat against the tribe's strongest brave.

Indians in league with the bad guys are always tricked into it. Once they discover they have been duped, they are more than happy to go on the warpath and help attack the villains (who may suddenly have many more bad guys of their own to nullify this advantage).

**Trick Shots:** White hats have an uncanny knack for firing their guns without ever killing anyone. Heroes gain +4 to any Task to shoot an object. This includes the gun in someone's hand, the cord holding the chandelier above the bad guy's head, and so on. The good guys cannot claim this bonus when shooting at zombies. Zombies are not considered objects.

Singing Cowboys can also make trick shots using ricochets and reflections in mirrors, pools, or glass. Each reflection or ricochet required subtracts -2 from the Task (far less than the modifier in any other genre—if such a shot would even be allowed). A hero who sees a dastardly villain sneaking up behind her while drinking from an oasis, for example, could fire her pistol at the large rock in front of her, have it bounce off the frying pan hanging on a wagon, then hit the villain smack in the gun.

# The Black Hats

Bad guys in the Singing Cowboys setting are thieves, bullies, and occasionally killers. They are not particularly vicious, however. They might slap someone around for information, but torture is right out. Maiming, mutilation, and rape are never committed in this genre.

There are three general types of bad guys (not counting zombies) in the Singing Cowboys genre: Goons, Hired Guns, and Bosses.

## Goons

Most bad guys are goons. Shoot the guns out of their hands and they run straight back to their boss. Goons never stop to pick up their prize firearms, but somewhere on the High Plains there must be an abundant supply, because they are always rearmed in the next scene. Goons are not very bright and even if they outnumber the good guys in a brawl, they usually attack one at a time.

A few goons may be a little more competent than others. These are usually foremen or lesser bosses that command groups of goons. They are a little tougher than the rest, and might occasionally do something clever (like getting other goons to pile on a hero and overwhelm her so the boss can place her in a death trap later).

Goons can be arrested after they get caught committing rough stuff. Unfortunately, they are almost always bailed out by their boss a short while after.

## Typical Goon

| | |
|---|---|
| **Strength** 2 | **Intelligence** 1 |
| **Dexterity** 2 | **Perception** 1 |
| **Constitution** 2 | **Willpower** 1 |
| **Life Points** 26 | **Speed** 8 |
| **Endurance Points** 20 | **Essence Pool** 9 |

**Drawbacks:** Cruel 1

**Skills:** Brawling 2, Cheating 1, Dodge 1, Guns (Any) 2, Intimidation 1, Notice 1, Riding (Horse) 2, Stealth 1, Swimming 1

**Gear:** Most goons carry pistols while in town, but keep rifles on their horses for battles in the wilderness.

## Typical Hired Gun

| | |
|---|---|
| **Strength** 2 | **Intelligence** 1 |
| **Dexterity** 4 | **Perception** 2 |
| **Constitution** 3 | **Willpower** 3 |
| **Life Points** 42 | **Speed** 14 |
| **Endurance Points** 29 | **Essence Pool** 14 |

**Qualities:** Fast as Heck, Fast Reaction Time, Hard to Kill 4, Nerves of Steel

**Drawbacks:** Cruel 2, Showoff, Status -1

**Skills:** Brawling 1, Cheating 3, Climbing 2, Demolitions 1, Dodge 3, Gambling 3, Guns (Handgun) 5, Guns (Rifle) 2, Guns (Shotgun) 2, Intimidation 3, Notice 2, Riding (horse) 3, Stealth 2, Swimming 1, Traps 2

**Gear:** Most hired guns carry pistols while in town, but keep rifles on their horses for battles in the wilderness.

## Hired Guns

Hired guns are a different breed than their employers or the incompetent goons who surround them. They are well-known gunfighters who sell their fast hands and deadly aim for a wad of cash.

Hired guns are not stupid, however, and they know to avoid run-ins with the law if at all possible. To keep the ropes from around their necks, hired guns never just draw down on heroes. They always attempt to goad their prey into an act of aggression first. That way the hired gun can claim a killing was self-defense and avoid the hangman's noose. To pull this off, the hired gun often "accidentally" runs into the white hats a few times before anything happens. In fact, hired guns know good guys do not fight unarmed foes and so often leave their weapons behind to avoid getting in a fight too early. Each time one of these encounters takes place and the hired gun walks away, he gains +1 to his Initiative and +2 Life Points when the final showdown takes place (up to a maximum of +6 in each). Losing face to a gunslinging bully scares those townsfolk who are depending on the hero—and has real game effects as well.

For all their ominous reputations, hired guns usually do not win. When one does, the good guy goes down and the gunslinger rides out of town before making sure his foe is dead. Of course, the hero is not dead. The bullet either just wounded her or more often it lodged miraculously in her badge, the Bible in her pocket, or the metal locket her sweetheart gave her in the previous scene.

Later, when a hero and the hired gun fight, the rules change a bit. Essentially, the good guy gets one freebie. After that she is fair game (at least by this hired gun's hand). Ignore the rule of Death for Singing Cowboys. This works both ways: a hero who cheated death once may now shoot to kill the hired gun with no penalty. The hero may regret having to kill, but she obviously has been left no choice and can lie in her bedroll at night with a clear conscience.

Hired guns never go quietly to jail unless they are sure the boss can release them (even a powerful rail baron cannot get a man out of jail for murder—but he could break him out if needed). Jail is not an option for these killers. They always fight to the bitter end.

## Bosses

The bosses in Singing Cowboys are the cattle kings, trail bosses, rail barons, and other town leaders responsible for whatever evil is taking place. They are the ones who are trying to scare everyone away from their claim-jumped mines, to run settlers off land that is about to be bought by the railroad, to kidnap the sheepfarmer's daughter, and so on. It usually takes the heroes a while to figure out what the bosses are up to even though their actions are apparent from the first. Sure, they are roughing up Old Man Miller and his ranch hands, but why?

Bosses are usually wealthy and powerful men (or very rarely, women). They cannot be arrested until the hero finds out every detail of their plan and comes up with proof of their evil deeds. "Proof" is a funny thing, however. A slip of the tongue in front of a lawman or other respected citizen, even if caused by some white hat's clever trick, is proof enough for the courts of the Singing Cowboys.

Bosses rarely arm themselves—that is what goons and hired guns are for. When they do pick up a gun, it is often to grab a hostage after their nefarious plans have been revealed. When that happens, heroes are allowed to go for a killing shot. Bosses know this, so they take their own lives in their hands when they pick up a six-shooter and attempt to use the Mayor's daughter to get out of town.

Fortunately for the heroes, bosses love death traps. They never just shoot captured heroes. They would much rather put one in a silo rapidly filling with grain then ride away, leaving the hero to "certain doom." Or tie one to a rickety chair near a bundle of dynamite with an incredibly long fuse. When truly pressed for time or creativity, the boss at least sends his toughest goon or hired gun to walk the hero far off his property and finish him. Of course, all of these death traps offer a hero plenty of opportunities for escape.

Bosses' love of death traps applies to the heroes' love interests as well. It is more satisfying to tie the Mayor's daughter to a railroad than it is to do anything truly nasty. Sidekicks and other companions are frequent targets of death traps as well.

## Zombies

No one is sure why the dead started waking in the land of the Singing Cowboys. One day, they just rose up out of the ground, groaning and looking for meat. The heroes do not mind too much, though. Most of them are frustrated that they can only shoot the guns out of the bad guys' hands anyway. Zombies are unnatural and do not have feelings, so it is okay to use all that fancy shooting to blast their hearts out.

What really bothers the heroes is that they cannot figure out just why the zombies have risen or what they are up to. They do not seem to have a plan, they attack at random and they do not really even do much damage. The oddest thing is that the townsfolk of the West, and even most heroes, just accept that they are now part of the story.

## What's Really Going On?

This one's weird, even for *All Flesh Must be Eaten*. The heroes in Singing Cowboys are not real. They are characters in Saturday morning matinee serials in the early 1950s. Unfortunately for them, science fiction monster movies are all the rage now. Since the writer/director behind this particular series has a lot of money riding on the show, he has decided to sell out and add a few zombies to his pictures. Frederick Ramirez could not think of any good way to work them into the plot—it just did not seem right to have his villains always raising zombies—so he just has them running amok in a couple of random night scenes. Ramirez is also fond of using his own name for many of the town's most important people. After a few adventures in which his very distinctive name keeps popping up, the players may start to catch on to the trick.

This is probably not the kind of campaign a Zombie Master wants to run for years, but it makes for an incredibly fun game to play for a couple of weeks until the players learn the secret. This is also why all those weird world rules allow the heroes so much leverage (like not worrying about dying most of the time).

## Typical Boss

| | |
|---|---|
| **Strength** 1 | **Intelligence** 3 |
| **Dexterity** 1 | **Perception** 2 |
| **Constitution** 1 | **Willpower** 3 |
| **Life Points** 18 | **Speed** 4 |
| **Endurance Points** 20 | **Essence Pool** 11 |

**Qualities:** Resources (Wealthy)

**Drawbacks:** Covetous (Greedy) 3, Obsession (Personal Power)

**Skills:** Brawling 1, Bureaucracy 3, Cheating 2, Gambling 3, Guns (Handgun) 2, Haggling 3, Intimidation 3, Notice 3, Questioning 2, Riding (Horse) 2, Smooth Talking 1, Traps 2

# Singing Cowboy Zombies

The dead featured in this genre are for the most part very generic. They are not very smart or very fast. They only come out at night and their weak spot is in their hearts (shooting something in the head is just too graphic for Ramirez' audience).

Corpses enter the scene only when the action seems slow. A fight with zombies, even if it takes place just outside the cattle baron's ranch house, rarely awakens the villains inside either, unless the Zombie Master wants it to.

# Story Ideas

The Singing Cowboy genre has few stories. That is part of the gag. The trick is changing the details from time to time and playing the joke for all it is worth. Since the heroes are actually characters in a movie, it is even appropriate to recycle props (Ramirez is on a budget, after all). A wagon with a jarring, lopsided wheel, a glass with a broken rim that nicks the hero's lips, or an Indian village that looks exactly like the last one the party visited may all clue the players in as to what is really happening. When that happens, their characters are welcome to make the leap of logic as well.

It is also appropriate to have the same actor play different extras. The villain in one episode could look just like the Town Marshal in the next. Of course, the extras are as oblivious to their status as the heroes, so they never understand what the "loco strangers" are talking about if confronted. Even if some sort of proof is given, such as the heroes dragging the villain from the last town over to the next and bringing him face-to-face with his double, the two will just nod a bit and say, "Yeah, I guess I can see a slight resemblance."

Here are a few of the most typical plots. The Zombie Master should also watch a few of the old Roy Rogers and Gene Autry serials for more inspiration (some are even available for free downloads on the web). The *Starz Western Channel* is also a rich source of 1930s features.

## Singing Cowboy Zombies

| | |
|---|---|
| **Strength** 1 | **Intelligence** -2 |
| **Dexterity** 1 | **Perception** 1 |
| **Constitution** 2 | **Willpower** 2 |
| **Dead Points** 15 | **Speed** 2 |
| **Endurance Points** n/a | **Essence Pool** 9 |

**Attack:** D4(2) slashing damage. Most zombies in Ramirez' flicks simply scratch and bite. Rarely do they pick up a gun or hand weapon.

**Weak Spot:** Heart (7)

**Getting Around:** Slow and Steady (0)

**Strength:** Ninety-Pound Weakling (-3)

**Senses:** Like the Dead (0); Scent Tracking (2)

**Sustenance:** Who Needs Food? (8)

**Intelligence:** Dumb as Dead Wood (0)

**Spreading the Love:** None (-3); Ramirez just creates more when he needs them

**Power:** 16

## Gentle as Lambs

In this classic story, the poor humble sheep farmers are being driven off their grazing land by the cattle kings or the rail barons. The Zombie Master can flip the three factions around occasionally, but usually it is the sheep farmers who are the innocents. Perhaps it is a reflection of Christianity or perhaps evil sheep farmers just seem too silly even for the genre.

The story goes something like this. The heroes wander into town and witness a gang of goons beating up a peaceful shepherd. The party comes to the shepherd's aid and the goons go to jail. Soon after, the boss (a cattle king) comes to town and bails out his boys. He also swears out a warrant against the shepherd. The goons claim he started the fight and since there are at least five of them, the sheriff cannot completely ignore them. To top it off, the boss says the sheep farmers keep trespassing on his land and the sheep are eating up the cattle's prime grazing grass. He insists the sheriff prosecute the sheep farmers and the lawman has no choice but to comply.

The sheep farmer swears he and the other herders do not let their sheep stray, but they keep showing up on the cattle king's land anyway. He suspects the bad guys rustle a sheep or two by night and carry them over onto the boss' land. The pasture is usually protected by barbed wire, but if the sheep farmer claims that is why his sheep couldn't trespass, the cattle king retorts that it only proves the shepherds are deliberately crossing onto his vast estates.

To prove the cattle king's crime, the party must catch some of his henchmen rustling sheep. This should take place at night. A few hours after the white hats begin their stakeout, zombies strike. The inexplicable attack lasts but a few minutes and when it is over, the characters may resume their stakeout. The villains, of course, do not hear the fight no matter how close they were when it happened.

Eventually, the bad guys show up, get caught and a gunfight ensues. After a few shots are fired, everyone somehow manages to move the fight into a big patch of rocks where amazing amounts of ammunition are expended and few people are hit. The goons eventually escape or are captured, and the sheriff swears to go after the boss. Inevitably, the sheriff is either wounded, cannot leave town, does not have jurisdiction, or must wait until the circuit judge comes to town. This gives the boss time to employ a hired gun, bail his boys out once more, and see if he can't get the strangers killed somehow.

One of the heroes, whoever has raised the cattle king's ire the most, is provoked by the hired gun. Verbal assaults are first, and then Sidekicks, love interests or friendly extras are insulted and bullied. If none of that works, one of the extras is kidnapped. If at all possible, this should lead to a showdown (see p. 33). If the hero draws first, for any reason, she violates the Law of the West and suffers accordingly. Should she continue to resist, the hired gun eventually calls her out and a duel results. To keep the rest of the party involved, the bad guys may well put a couple of shooters in nearby windows as well.

## Claim Jumping

In this tale, the party is traveling the high desert of the southwest when they come across a body riddled with arrows. They take the body to town for a decent Christian burial and find out the man was a local prospector that everyone simply called . . . the Prospector. Some—the goons of a local boss (cattle king, rail baron, mine owner, banker, or other wealthy individual)—say the Prospector was always trespassing on Indian lands and got what he deserved. Others say the Prospector swore he was onto something big and might have even filed a claim. A check at the local mining office proves no claim was filed, but the nervous clerk there is actually on the take of the local villain.

The heroes inevitably become nosey and the goons come to rough them up. They do not talk, but in the aftermath, the town drunk, noble saloon gal, or dying townsperson says she saw the Prospector digging around some notable landmark (Devil's Creek, Black Rock, Blood Ridge, or some other suitably ominous place) far outside of town. The heroes venture to the site but do not find it until twilight. They stumble across a recently dug mine shaft and

some scattered tools, then find a pair of weathered saddlebags lying in the brush. Inside is a deed signed by the town's mining office and made out to the Prospector. He had filed a claim after all. The party is likely just about to ride back to town with their proof when the zombies appear—right between the heroes and their horses.

The inevitable fight ensues before the heroes make their way back to town. The sheriff has his hands full with a group of rowdy trail hands, but hires on the party as deputies and sends them to the boss' ranch to bring him in. There the heroes meet the hired gun, but he is unarmed. He claims he just arrived and his employer is not home. Taunting ensues, giving the hired gun a chance to wear down the hero that riles him the most. Later, when the heroes have ridden off, the hired gun finds his employer. The boss then sends his new henchman into town after the "goody two-shoes troublemakers."

Back in town, the heroes have to help the sheriff fend off the rowdy trail hands. Somewhere in the ruckus, they cross paths with the boss's goons and his hired gun. The situation eventually ends with a gunfight. The goons run for a boardwalk full of barrels and crates piled along Main Street while the hired gun calls out whichever hero he has become particularly annoyed by. While chaos ensues, these two have a classic showdown.

The next day, the heroes find out the boss has fled for Mexico. They immediately set off after her, running across more wandering bands of zombies before eventually trapping the bad guys in a box canyon.

## Iron Horses

The next story concerns the coming of the railroad and its steam-powered "iron horses." This time, the heroes find a town plagued by bad men. Scores of goons and likely several hired guns ride roughshod over the town, terrorizing decent folks with guns and fists. The criminals stand by each other so that few crimes can be proven and the new sheriff (the last three were killed mysteriously) just does not know what to do. He offers bounties to the heroes if they help him make the town a decent place for folks to live again.

Singing Cowboys

Most folks have left, he claims, but at the very least the local cattle king has given them something for their land so that they did not lose everything.

Over the next few days, the new deputies patrol the town, round up the bad guys, and do their best to serve up some law and order. Needless to say, the cattle king is behind everything. When confronted, however, he denies it all and several prominent townsfolk stand with him. Still, the boss becomes worried and tells his agents to step up the violence. Eventually, several of the hired guns, who have played it cool up to now, find excuses to call out the new lawmen. The worst might even try an ambush or attempt to lure the white hats into a death trap.

One night, the heroes see a strange light coming from Boot Hill. Investigating, they see a man with surveyor's tools taking measurements by moonlight on the high hill. As they are about to close in, the surveyor is dragged beneath the desert floor by the hands of the walking dead. The heroes find themselves on the inside of a fenced-in graveyard with a passel of risen fiends.

When the fight eventually ends, the party opens the surveyor's kit and finds that he works for the Union-Pacific Railroad. Also in his bag is a map showing a proposed train route smack through the town. Whoever owns the various shops, stock, and land will be rich.

Confronted with this evidence, the cattle king is brought to justice and the heroes ride into the setting sun.

## Indian War

The local Indians are on the warpath. They have been chasing stages, raiding outlying farms, and generally terrorizing "civilized" folks. Four local businessmen clamor for the Indians' blood, claiming their attacks are costing not only lives, but the hard-earned dollars of the local citizens as well. The sheriff has no choice but to send a telegram to the cavalry and ask them to come round up the hostiles.

Fortunately, one of the heroes knows something about the Indians. She might even have a contact

there. The party ventures into the desert and attempts to find the tribe. The search takes all night and the good guys find they have accidentally ridden into an ancient Indian burial ground. Like clockwork, the dead arise—bursting from the ground or climbing down off their burial scaffolds. Battle ensues, and just as the heroes blast the last zombie, the Indian tribe shows up and surrounds them.

A tense meeting ensues, but cooler heads prevail and the Indians say they are only retaliating for attacks by the white men, who have been riding through their village shooting people at random. A description of one of the bad white men matches that of a well-known hired gun who just happens to be staying at the local hotel. The heroes also notice the Indians have brand new guns. If pressed, the natives reveal they bought them with gold from white traders. The description of the traders just happens to match the four businessmen calling for the "savages' blood."

The heroes ride back to town, now knowing that the businessmen in town have stirred up a war in order to sell guns to both sides. Perhaps one of the heroes even noticed the same type of gun sold to the Indians in large supply at one of the men's stores. These would be sold to any posse rounded up to war with the Indians.

Three of the businessmen are quickly rounded up and confess to their crimes. The fourth, however, somehow got word that the heroes were on to him and fled town with his goons and the hired gun who has been shooting Indians. The heroes pursue the well-armed band out into the badlands and after another nighttime encounter with the walking dead, find and defeat the black hats.

The finale is completed as the Indians arrive, seeking vengeance by death. The heroes must then defend their captives from the Indians and must do so without letting a fight with the unfortunate tribe break out.

# Wrapping it Up

When the Zombie Master has run each of the four plots above, she should run one of them again—but with different details (as explained above). After a few repeats, the players should catch on to what is going on. This is the point at which the audience begins to lose interest. Ramirez is given one more episode to draw back in the customers. He decides to go all out. All of the heroes' old villains return from the dead. They retain their old personalities and skills with the enhanced abilities of the walking dead from this genre. As many regular zombies as the Zombie Master sees fit accompany them.

If the heroes survive the fight, Ramirez was successful and gets to keep making his movies. If they fail, he wraps up the series with this depressing ending and fades into obscurity. In either case, it is likely time to end the campaign. The Zombie Master should tell the survivors that they ride off into the sunset in their final episode. The dead are given decent burials and a solemn ballad by the survivors (or another Singing Cowboy if none saw the sun set this day).

# Singing Cowboy
## Survivor

**Str** 4 **Dex** 4 **Con** 3
**Int** 3 **Per** 3 **Wil** 3
**LPs** 53
**EPs** 35
**Spd** 14
**Essence** 20

## Qualities/Drawbacks

Charisma +4 (4)
Fast as Heck (1)
Fast Reaction Time (2)
Hard to Kill 5 (5)
Honorable (-3)
Law of the West (-5)
Reckless (-2)
Wonder Horse (3)

## Skills

Brawling 5
Dancing 2
First Aid 2
Guns (Handgun) 5
Guns (Rifle) 4
Hand Weapon (Lasso) 3
Notice 3
Play Instrument (Guitar) 5
Research/Investigation 2
Riding 5
Singing 5
Stealth 1
Survival (Desert) 2
Tracking 1

## Gear

Comet the Wonder Horse,
Colt Peacemaker with
24 Bullets, Lasso

## Personality

To the tune of "Red River Valley."

In this valley they say there are zombies,
Walking dead with no pulse and no smile,
No one knows how they rose from the graveyard,
But I ace them with grace and with style.

Come and sit by my side if you see them,
I'll protect you from
all that you fear,
Just remember to
not let them bite you,
And aim true, shoot the
heart out, my dear.

## Quote

"Comet! To me, boy!"

# Singing Cowgirl
## Survivor

**Str** 2 **Dex** 3 **Con** 3
**Int** 4 **Per** 4 **Wil** 4
**LPs** 45
**EPs** 32
**Spd** 12
**Essence** 20

## Qualities/Drawbacks
Attractiveness +3 (3)
Charisma +2 (2)
Fast Reaction Time (2)
Hard to Kill 5 (5)
Honorable (-3)
Law of the West (-5)
Secret (In Love
with Singing Cowboy) (-2)
Wonder Horse (3)

## Skills
Acting 3
Brawling 2
Dancing (Square) 2
Dodge 3
First Aid 4
Guns (Handgun) 4
Guns (Rifle) 4
Guns (Shotgun) 3
Intimidation 2
Notice 3
Research/Investigation 2
Riding (Horse) 4
Singing 4
Smooth Talking 2
Stealth 3

## Gear
Midnight the Wonder Horse,
Winchester '76 Rifle, 50 shells,
Trunk (full of rawhide dresses,
both practical and respectable)

## Personality
To the tune of "My Darlin' Clementine."

Oh my darlin',
Oh my darlin',
Oh my darlin', love of mine,
You are lost and gone forever,
Zombies killed you in a mine.

I should have warned you,
Should have cried out,
Should have screamed, and
drawn my gun,
But you said "Now stand back
darlin',"
You were havin' so much fun.

Then that big one,
With the pickaxe,
Snuck up on you in the dark,
Then you would have been one of them,
But I shot you in the heart.

## Quote
"Oh, Rex! That was beautiful!"

Singing Cowboys

# CHAPTER FOUR

TRUE GRIT

# "There, Marshal Coghill! That's the cave drawn on my husband's map. I'm sure they're in there somewhere."

United States Marshal Henry "Hawk" Coghill looked down the red rock valley to a tiny black opening at the base of a massive mesa. His gray hair, eye patch, and rough clothes said much about his 30 years serving the United States—first in the Army and now as a Marshal. He grunted to show he'd seen it, then spurred his gray mare on down the rocky hill.

Penelope Miller, pretty young wife of Professor Darren Miller, followed. Her petticoats were covered in dust and her parasol was tattered, but she still carried herself like she was attending a governor's inauguration.

Coghill looked back with his good eye to make sure she rode her pony down the hillside, but turned his gaze away quickly when she looked his way. "Come on," he bellowed, as if she were holding him back. He'd told her not to come, but the stubborn schoolmarm would have none of that. Her Darren was in trouble and she'd purge the depths of Hell if she thought it would help. Little did she know that's just where she was going.

The Marshal reigned up outside the cave. His friend, an old Hunkpapa Sioux he called simply "Tracker," looked up at the sky. "Going to be dark soon. Bad time to trespass on Anasazi ground."

"Ana-who?" Coghill grunted as he climbed down off his horse. He took some equipment off the animal's back—some rope, a lantern, and a pickaxe.

"Anasazi. Old ones. They just up and disappeared long ago. No one knows why." Tracker looked up at the sky again. "Bad time to trespass."

"You said that. Now let's go. See any tracks here?"

Tracker nodded. "Four go in. Twenty or more come out."

Coghill gave the old Indian a one-eyed glare. "I thought you said the Anasazi were dead?"

Tracker nodded. "They are."

\* \* \*

The cavern was narrow and long, and there were signs of recent activity by Professor Miller and his three-man team. After a good fifty yards, the tunnel opened up into a massive cathedral-like room. Against the far wall, barely visible by Coghill's torchlight, was a sheer cliff face with zigzagging stairs climbing its height. Penelope started toward the stairs but Coghill stepped on the train of her dress.

"Watch your big, clumsy . . ." Penelope looked to the Marshal and saw him squinting up at the top of the stairs. She followed his gaze and gasped in horror when she saw a human hand protruding from one of the uppermost steps. "Darren?" she whispered.

Coghill shrugged. He pulled a shotgun from his bag full of tools, then handed the sack and his torch to Tracker. Slowly and quietly for a man of his girth and swagger, he climbed the long stairs. When he reached a point where he could see just who possessed the hand, he charged.

The corpse was a few weeks old. Half eaten, disgusting, but no threat.

The Marshal looked above the cliff shelf and rubbed his remaining eye in disbelief. An entire city lay before him. "Tracker," he called as quietly as possible. "Come on up. And bring a blanket. Ms. Miller, you come up thirty paces behind." The two did as instructed. Marshal Coghill used the blanket to hide the grisly remains. It wasn't Professor Miller, but it was one of his three companions.

Penelope looked down at the covered corpse, then up at Coghill. "Is it?"

"No. It isn't," he replied as he helped her step over the gruesome find.

The trio walked cautiously down the main street that ran down through the hidden city. Dark shadows flickered in their small torchlight. "Dark is a bad time to trespass," Tracker reminded.

"We're underground, Injun," Coghill answered, annoyed. "Gonna be just as dark down here at high noon as at midnight."

"Not worried about light. Time. Anasazi more powerful at night."

"Why didn't you tell me that?" Coghill glared.

"Did."

"Not hardly!"

"I said, 'dark is a bad time to trespass on . . .'"

"I know what you said, you durned fool! But you didn't . . . aw, never mind. Let's find this tinhorn and get outta here."

Marshal Coghill shot Mrs. Miller a glance. "No offense meant, ma'am."

"None taken, Marshal," she huffed as she walked past him and into the ruins.

A little further into the city, Penelope spotted the remains of a campsite. "Look!" she said louder than either of her companions liked. "They were here! This was their base camp!" Penelope's excitement died quickly when she saw the disheveled ruins of the tent, bedrolls, and camping gear.

Tracker walked into the middle of the mess and shook his head. "Someone tore up camp, but didn't take anything."

Coghill nodded. He looked around, slowly. The towering stone buildings above him contained scores of windows. The shadows given by the torchlight seemed to dance, suggesting hidden figures in every one.

"Look! There!" Penelope shouted, again far too loud. She ran further into the city to what must have once been a great temple. "Look at all the picks and hammers. These doors must have been sealed. Quick, Marshal! Bring the torch!"

Coghill grunted but followed the schoolmarm into the ruin. The moment he crossed the threshold, he got a sinking feeling. Strange symbols had been painted into the walls, the ceiling, and the floors. Old bones, perhaps thousands of years old, lay scattered about the floor. Judging by the skulls, they were human.

Tracker stood in the doorway and frowned. "Look at the mortar on the steps outside. These doors weren't sealed to keep people out. They were sealed to keep something in."

Coghill felt the hair on the back of his neck rise. "Let's get outta here," he said. Tracker was already half down the steps, but Penelope hesitated. "Come on," he repeated.

"No! Darren may be in here somewhere! I'm not leaving these ruins just because you and that superstitious Indian are afraid of the dark!"

Coghill saw shambling forms move in the darkness of the vast temple. "Now!" he ordered.

"And if you think yelling at me is going to make any difference—"

Coghill grabbed Penelope and threw her over his shoulder. She screamed and flailed on his strong back helplessly. "Put me down!" Something made a noise behind the pair and Penelope raised her head. Rushing from the shadows were hideous forms—Indians by the look of them, but the withered husks and bared teeth revealed they had died long since. "Faster!" she screamed.

Coghill and Tracker raced through the town as groaning undead arose from the shadowed doorways. Tracker fired first, blowing one's head off with his Winchester '73. He cocked the lever calmly as he pressed on, selectively shooting only those ancient dead that blocked their way out.

Coghill saw two close in behind Tracker. He dumped Penelope on her rear in front of him and blasted the things with both barrels. They shattered in a cloud of dust and mold. Penelope screamed, sat up and drew the Marshal's pistol from his holster. She fired, smack between his legs. His one wide-eye glared at her, terrified to look down and see exactly what she had done. From what he could see, all was still intact. He whirled, finally realizing she was firing at something behind him and saw a wave of rushing undead. Dusty, dried corpses raced down the temple steps and from the dark alleyways of the city. Hawk dropped the shotgun behind him along with a box of shells. "Reload it!" he yelled as he snatched the pistol from her hand and started blazing.

Tracker ran back toward them, throwing in his lot with the pale-faces. It was a poor decision. A ravenous zombie leapt from a window and landed atop him, tearing into the quiet Indian with its ancient teeth.

Coghill grimaced and gunned the thing down, but it was too late. Tracker kept firing until he was empty, then rolled over and died.

"Marshal!" Penelope handed him the shotgun.

"Hang on!" Coghill yelled. He scooped Penelope up with one hand and blasted a pair of zombies with the other. Then he dropped the shotgun and picked up the torch. "We'll burn our way out!" he grunted in anger.

Coghill barreled his way toward the exit, bashing a dusty undead in the arm with his brand. The thing caught fire instantly, then began to scream in an unholy voice. The howls of the first creature slowed the rest and gave Coghill time to make the entrance. He slowed there and put Penelope down. "Untie the horses!" he ordered. "I'll hold them at the entrance."

Penelope did as she was told and soon came up with all three animals.

Coghill drew the rifle off his horse and threw it to Penelope. "Hold 'em for a minute," he grunted. The Marshal began to rifle through his saddlebags.

Penelope fired off a half-dozen shots. Most of the rounds seemed to have little effect, but one caught a corpse in the head and stopped it for good.

Finally, Marshal Coghill smiled. "Found it," he said. He turned with one stick of dynamite in his hand and lit it with the dying torch. "Go back to Hell," he yelled at the hordes of things gathered in the tunnel. He tossed the dynamite in then turned his back. Penelope caught herself staring at the cave, then finally realized what was about to happen and dove to the ground.

A massive blast echoed from the tunnel. Dust, dirt, stone, and bone flew from the entrance and peppered the heroes and their horses. Thousand of tons of earth collapsed all along the length of the old opening, burying countless undead in its wake.

When the rumbling stopped and the dust cleared, Marshal Coghill looked up at the dazed young schoolmarm. "Your husband's dead. I saw him back there. I'm sorry, ma'am."

Penelope was dazed. The shock of seeing the walking dead outweighed the grief she felt for her fallen husband. For the moment. "Yes," she finally nodded.

What Coghill hadn't told her was that her husband, like the old Anasazi, had joined the ranks of the damned. He had been in the pack at the tunnel mouth. "I don't know what we just saw. How it could be. But at least we sealed them up in there. Forever."

Penelope nodded quietly, but somehow, she knew he was wrong.

# Introduction

True Grit is a Western setting reminiscent of the John Wayne movies, particularly those of the late 1960s and 1970s. Men are men and women are annoying companions (or at least they are treated as such). Swagger, intimidation, and toughness are more important than a fast gun. A cowboy who gets shot has to have the sand to tough it out and drive on until the fight is over. Only then is he allowed to die.

# Making Characters

John Wayne-type heroes in True Grit are tough hombres. They are tough to kill and never say die until they are actually dead.

Other characters usually play second fiddle to those with True Grit, but can be just as interesting to play. "Citified" folks, particularly women, add great contrast to the party and give those with True Grit something to complain and grumble about. Inventors with new-fangled motorcycles or horseless carriages (if played in the later periods of the West) or special weapons are often seen in these movies as well.

Indian characters make excellent Cast Members in this genre. These men and women are usually former Army scouts, the last of their tribes or otherwise detached from their people, and so can freely travel about the plains without worrying about tribal obligations. Of course, these Cast Members prove extremely helpful when their people are encountered and are a hindrance when entering white-dominated towns.

## Recommended Qualities and Drawbacks

Hard to Kill is very appropriate, especially when combined with True Grit (see p. 60).

Any Drawbacks that make a character grumpy, cantankerous, and otherwise hostile are also appropriate. Such flaws are always superficial, however. Any hero worth his salt is also loyal to his companions, no matter how much he pretends not to like them.

# New Qualities and Drawbacks

## True Grit

### 3-point Physical Quality

A character with "True Grit" has what old-timers call "sand." The son of a bitch is so tough he just will not die until he has had his way. He can take an incredible amount of damage and while it hurts him just as much as anyone else, he does not show it until his task is finished, the innocent are saved or his companions have escaped what would otherwise be certain death. The cowboy might complain louder than a three-legged mule while driving on death's door, but only to his friends. He never lets his opponents see his pain.

When the good fight is over, a wounded hero with True Grit is either waiting on a doctor's care (which he always mistrusts) or the undertaker.

In game terms, characters with True Grit can keep fighting even when their Life Points reach zero. Every round after Life Points equal zero, no matter how low they go, the character can continue to act as long as he passes a Simple Willpower Test. The Zombie Master can override this rule for special situations, but in the normal course of events, the hero just keeps on going.

Once the character has completed his goal, he succumbs to his wounds normally. The hero's "goal" depends on the situation. For instance, a cowboy with True Grit who stays at the throttle of a locomotive loaded with zombies so he can make sure it derails into a deep ravine a few miles distant is a good example. Another might be a cowboy who covers his party's exit from a deep cave while he stays behind to light a bundle of dynamite. The Zombie Master has final say on what eventually makes the hero drop, but it should always be dramatic. The player should grumble, complain, and curse the whole time for proper effect.

# The Dead Arise

True Grit takes place in the later period of the West, sometime after 1880. The Zombie Master should feel free to bump the era up into the late 1880s or even 1890s if he would like to have crude automobiles and other inventions present (see the John Wayne movie *Big Jake* for a great treatment of this concept).

The story begins when an ancient evil is awakened by an unfortunate explorer. This intrepid gent was searching for an answer to the great mystery of the Anasazi, a legendary tribe of Indians that disappeared many centuries before white men ever crossed the plains. The awakened evil grows by creating legions of undead—both human and animal. If the heroes don't stop the creature, it will eventually turn the entire West—and maybe the world—into a vast charnel house.

## Secrets of the Anasazi

In 1876 (or later, if moving the era forward), four explorers wandered deep into ancient Anasazi ruins. Within the thousand-year old depths of the long-dead city, they discovered a great and terrible secret. The Anasazi had been fierce warriors, but it was their mastery of the black arts that had terrified their rivals. What few knew was that the source of the Anasazi sorcerers' power was a potent elder thing they called Kinatuk—"Blood Thing." Kinatuk was unfortunate enough to be caught by the only tribe capable of such a feat, for the Anasazi had been instructed by other creatures from beyond the stars long ago.

The Anasazi lured the thing into one of their ancient cities and sacrificed their own people in a murderous ritual to bind it. Trapped in a city of the dead, Kinatuk became the power source for the Anasazi's incredible sorcery. Soon the armies of the Anasazi rode forth and conquered the plains. Thousands of what would later be called "Indians" fell before them and became slaves to these now-forgotten people.

But the Anasazi sorcerers became too greedy. One day they attempted to conduct a massive ritual that would make all their people immortal. The Blood Thing gave the sorcerers all they wanted—channeling all of its incredible energy through them and their people. The foolish Anasazi screamed as their blood boiled and cooked them from the inside out. They collapsed as withered husks, their race consumed in one eldritch act of genocide. Any human who was more than half Anasazi combusted in a fiery, scarlet fountain of burning blood.

The Blood Thing collapsed as well—not dead, but dormant within its mystic bonds. There it has lain until the day Dr. Darren Miller excavated the Anasazi temple and despoiled the elder signs that held it in place.

Even in its weakened form, Kinatuk made short work of the poorly armed expedition and supped upon their warm blood to restore its strength. The creature then erupted from the cave in a rage, leaving behind the animated remains of its captors as punishment for their crimes against it.

Kinatuk now wanders the vast prairies, slaying those it comes across to feed its thousand-year-old appetite. But the creature realizes the world is very different than it was a millennium ago. Should it show itself too soon, humans might band together and kill it—or worse, these primitive "monkeys" might once again bind it in eternal slavery. The Blood Thing has vowed this will not happen again. It will die first.

To prevent either possibility, Kinatuk uses its eldritch powers to spread its essence among those it kills. It drains their life force through a terrifying, biting kiss, then breathes out a small portion of its own energy back into the corpse. That creature rises as the walking dead and carries a small piece of Kinatuk inside it. Because of this mystical link, the creature's shambling hordes share a similar characteristic—they bleed from the mouth constantly. The red gore drains down their throats and into their clothes, making them more grisly and frightening than usual.

Animals, too, can become part of the Blood Thing's horde. At least two rotting buffalo herds now wander the prairies of the West and grisly, tireless buzzards keep watch over from high overhead. Wolves have also become undead minions of the

Blood Thing. These indefatigable hunters stalk lone settlers across the plains, waiting for an unguarded moment to strike.

Kinatuk's minions are spread far and wide. The dispersal allows the Blood Thing to quietly and quickly ravage the West without attracting too much attention in one place. Most of Kinatuk's minions travel in groups of 8-28 (2D10 + 8) for people or buffalo. Wolves operate in packs of 1-10 (D10).

The Blood Thing's own "bodyguard" consists of 2D10 + 20 minions, many of which are armed with firearms or hand weapons such as pitchforks or cavalry sabers.

It has also left behind a small retinue of servants in the cave in which it was once bound. These servants are to guard the city and prevent other monkeys from uncovering any ancient knowledge that might be found there.

## The Zombies

Most of the dead created by Kinatuk are "Mouth Bleeders." These are the humans and animals the Blood Thing has placed its essence into to protect it from those who might learn its secret. They aren't particularly fast, but they are savage and cunning. Also, like their master, they hate human monkeys, except to feast upon. The Blood Thing's zombies are extensions of it—they don't use guns but are happy to pick up any hand weapons they find available—the more barbs, tines, or nicks to make bloody wounds with, the better. Those with professions are able to remember some of their tricks in undeath. Trappers, for instance, might carry a few traps with them and know how to use them. Hunters and gunslingers might carry firearms, and a farmer might carry a pitchfork. Such individuals are rare, however. Usually only one in any pack of minions is so gifted.

Mouth Bleeders drain a few pints of blood through the victim's mouth but leave the corpse intact so that it may join the pack. Kinatuk can do this as well, but seein' as that creature is nearly insatiable, its prey is usually reduced to a withered mass incapable of effective animation.

### Mouth Bleeders

| | |
|---|---|
| **Strength** 4 | **Intelligence** -2 |
| **Dexterity** 2 | **Perception** 1 |
| **Constitution** 2 | **Willpower** 2 |
| **Dead Points** 15 | **Speed** 4 |
| **Endurance Points** n/a | **Essence Pool** 9 |

**Skills:** Usually none, but may vary

**Attack:** Bite D4 x 2(4) slashing damage

**Weak Spot:** Brain (6)

**Getting Around:** Life-like (3); The Lunge (3)

**Strength:** Strong like Bull (5)

**Senses:** Like the Dead (0); Scent Tracking (1)

**Sustenance:** Occasionally (2); Blood (-2)

**Intelligence:** Dumb as Dead Wood (but see the special notes on Kinatuk, p. 75)

**Spreading the Love:** Special (2)

**Power:** 25

## Mouth Bleeder Buffalo

**Strength** 6     **Intelligence** -2

**Dexterity** 1     **Perception** 1

**Constitution** 2     **Willpower** 2

**Dead Points** 15     **Speed** 6

**Endurance Points** n/a     **Essence Pool** 10

**Skills:** Usually none, but may vary

**Attack:** Gore D4 x 6(12) slashing damage (3)

**Weak Spot:** Brain (6)

**Getting Around:** Special (1)

**Strength:** Special (7)

**Senses:** Like the Dead (0); Scent Tracking (1)

**Sustenance:** Occasionally (2); Blood (-2)

**Intelligence:** Dumb as Dead Wood (but see the special notes on Kinatuk, p. 75)

**Spreading the Love:** Special (2; having a five-hundred pound buffalo do this generally causes the corpse great disfigurement)

**Power:** 25

## Mouth Bleeder Wolves

**Strength** 2     **Intelligence** -2

**Dexterity** 2     **Perception** 3

**Constitution** 2     **Willpower** 2

**Dead Points** 15     **Speed** 8

**Endurance Points** n/a     **Essence Pool** 9

**Skills:** Usually none, but may vary

**Attack:** Bite D4 x 2(4) slashing damage

**Weak Spot:** Brain (6)

**Getting Around:** Special (2)

**Strength:** Dead Joe Average (0)

**Senses:** Like the Dead (0); Scent Tracking (3)

**Sustenance:** Occasionally (2); Blood (-2)

**Intelligence:** Dumb as Dead Wood (but see the special notes on Kinatuk, p. 75)

**Spreading the Love:** Special (2)

**Power:** 18

### Spreading the Love

Kinatuk's minions use a form of One Bite and You're Hooked to spread the love. Mouth Bleeders make new zombies by performing a biting kiss that literally gnaws the victim's lips off. This can only be done only once a victim is helpless—not in combat.

True Grit

## Anasazi Undead

The final ritual of the Anasazi bound them blood and soul with Kinatuk. Through that bond, the creature has been able to resurrect the Anasazi corpses that remained near its prison. These horrors are far more powerful than the Mouth Bleeders the Blood Thing has recently created and altogether different as well. They do not bleed from the mouth and their bodies remain the dried-up husks they were when the ritual first slew them. There are more mummies than zombies (at least so far), but their hatred for the living makes them nearly indistinguishable from the title-villains of this game.

Anasazi undead ravage flesh out of pure hatred, but don't actually draw sustenance from it.

## Kinatuk

The Blood Thing appears as a massive (nine-foot tall) humanoid covered with bloody veins, ropey arteries and beating, exposed organs. Its crimson eyes stand out on its dull head like two congealed drops of dimpled blood. It has no mouth and its hands end in ragged, flaying arteries that spew dark and gory blood.

Fitting for the big nasty of the tale, Kinatuk has several special abilities.

**Blood Drain:** Kinatuk literally leaches blood from any warm-blooded creature within five yards (meters). These victims automatically lose one Life Point each Turn. Only someone in a sealed, airtight, hardened suit can resist this effect. The technology is probably not available in this era, however.

**Blood Slap:** Those hit by the creature's flailing veins (arms) lose D6 x 4(12) Life Points. Hard armor (such as iron plates) protects against this damage, but leather chaps and other cloth do not (the blood drains straight through). A rain slicker or other treated garment reduces the damage to D6 x 2(6) Life Points.

**Blood Spray:** A constant blood spray emanating from Kinatuk hands and any veins or arteries severed in the fight. The spray clouds eyes and makes weapons and footing slippery, so characters within five yards (meters) of the thing must subtract -2 from all physical Task rolls.

## Anasazi Undead

| | |
|---|---|
| **Strength** 7 | **Intelligence** 2 |
| **Dexterity** 3 | **Perception** 2 |
| **Constitution** 4 | **Willpower** 3 |
| **Dead Points** 15 | **Speed** 18 |
| **Endurance Points** n/a | **Essence Pool** 21 |

**Skills:** Usually none, but may vary

**Attack:** Bite D4 x 2(4) slashing damage

**Weak Spot:** Brain (6)

**Getting Around:** The Quick Dead (10)

**Strength:** Monstrous Strength (10)

**Senses:** Like the Living (1); Life Sense (4)

**Sustenance:** Who Needs Food? (8)

**Intelligence:** Problem Solving (15)

**Spreading the Love:** None (victims of the Anasazi are often raised by attendant Mouth Bleeders instead)

**Special Zombie Features:** Spitter (2); Special Constitution and Willpower (3)

**Power:** 64

As Kinatuk is wounded, the blood spray becomes even more dramatic. A half-dead Blood Thing resembles a grotesque fountain of blood. The penalty inflicted by the creature's blood spray is increased to -3 when it has lost half its Life Points, and -4 when it is down to a quarter of its original points.

**Create Mouth Bleeders:** Kinatuk is not a zombie, nor even undead. It can create zombies, however, with a simple wave of its "hand." This requires a single action and raises 2D6 corpses if that many are available. The Blood Thing does not "summon" these beings—the corpses must be within 10 yards for this power to work.

Once created, Kinatuk can see and sense through all of the undead it or its minions have created. Being able to access their senses is not the same as being omniscient, however. There are now so many minions that Kinatuk is slow to focus its attention even when its creatures are being destroyed. This occurs D10 combat rounds after the first zombie in a pack is slain. At that point, the Blood Thing shifts its focus to another nearby corpse and directs the attack of the pack. The minions fight much more intelligently at this point and each gain five additional Dead Points as well.

When Kinatuk is active in a pack, the minions can speak in a crude, halting tongue. Their abilities are limited, so no particularly clever lies are told, but they can trick unsuspecting characters if they somehow hide their gruesome features. This is how Kinatuk gathers information, tricks passengers onto trains or stages filled with its minions, and so on.

Kinatuk does not necessarily chase down humans who attack its creatures. Only should a group show a determined effort to wipe out the Blood Thing and its minions does Kinatuk change its tactics. Most monkeys look alike to the thing, but it does remember faces after a few encounters in which it loses its minions. At that point, it dedicates one or more of its hordes to hunt the heroes down and slay them. A pack of undead wolves are often sent to find the hunters and soften them up. A few buffalo and a pack of Mouth Bleeders follow not too far behind.

Kinatuk is impossible to slay as long as its minions walk the earth. If "killed," the Blood Thing's con-sciousness lies dormant for 2D10 + 10 hours. After that, it flies to one of its many minions. Transferring to a minion is difficult for the Blood Thing, however. Each attempt requires two Success Levels at a Difficult Willpower Test. If Kinatuk is unsuccessful, the vessel is flawed in some way and cannot house its enormous spirit. If it is successful, the vessel begins to bleed, contort, and transmogrify. After D4 + 2 minutes and a spectacular shower of blood and gore, Kinatuk stands in its true form as before.

As long as Kinatuk has vessels it has not yet attempted and failed to inhabit, it has a way to escape and return to haunt the Cast Members another day.

### Kinatuk

**Strength** 10      **Intelligence** 6
**Dexterity** 3      **Perception** 5
**Constitution** 12      **Willpower** 6
**Life Points** 98      **Speed** 30
**Endurance Points** 89      **Essence Pool** 42
**Attacks:** Blood Drain, Blood Slap, Blood Spray, Create Mouth Bleeders

# Starting the Campaign

The heroes of True Grit should not know the dead walk at first. They should first play a more traditional "John Wayne" type adventure. Perhaps they are after gold stolen back during the War or they are attempting to recover a girl captured by Comanche raiders. At some point, late one night, they should come across a grisly scene—a camp full of dead travelers lies bleeding on the plains. They've been gnawed upon (by animals, not the dead), and this should, for the moment, hide the horrible bite marks upon their lips unless a character makes a Difficult Perception Test.

Later on, the heroes are attacked by what seems to be a half-dead rabid buffalo. Of course, the thing is undead, but characters are not likely to know that unless one of them is a doctor. Simply describe the creature as severely wounded—likely driven mad by its wounds or perhaps even by rabies.

The next encounter should be a completely normal fight with no strangeness, though the Zombie Master might make the heroes think otherwise. The trick is to keep them constantly guessing. If the adventure is about Indians, for example, a war party of braves might attack in the middle of the night. The braves have painted their bodies with ash and soot to look like the dead. The heroes will likely think they are zombies until they start grappling with them and realize they're warm-blooded and far too cunning to be undead.

Later on, a real party of undead attacks. The Zombie Master should not be afraid to let one of the Cast Members die if his number comes up. Though unfortunate, this is survival horror. The sudden realization that the world is not what the rest of the group thought, coupled with the death of one of their own, should drive the horror home with a bone spike.

## Vision Quest

If one of the characters is an Indian, he should get nicked by one of the zombies in their first encounter. If no one is an Indian, or has Indian blood, the Zombie Master can target a Mexican character instead. Failing that, the hero who was most wounded in the attack (make sure at least one person gets mauled) receives an inexplicable vision caused by a small infection in his blood.

The night of the attack, the chosen character develops a terrible fever from his wound (no matter how light) and experiences a vision. In it, an ancient shaman tells him the story of Kinatuk, and how the blood thing now spreads its essence among all those it raises from the dead. The character should awake in a bloody sweat, his wounds healed and his fever broken. He should then tell the rest of the group what he saw and the campaign to chase down Kinatuk and all its minions can begin.

Another way to introduce the information about Kinatuk is to have a companion (or loved one) of the lost Miller expedition hire the party to escort them to the Anasazi ruins. There, some egghead in the group can decipher the ancient pictographs and discover the Blood Thing's secrets. The rest of the party likely makes fun of the "tinhorn" professors until the Anasazi undead attack and convince them of Kinatuk's unholy existence.

## The Campaign

After the initial encounter and either a vision quest or a trip to the Anasazi ruins, the heroes should know that Kinatuk exists. They should also realize it must be destroyed or the entire world will one day be nothing but a seething mass of mouth-bleeding undead. Unfortunately, to slay the Blood Thing, the heroes must kill almost every single undead horror it has created. That's a tall order. Tracking them all down is extremely difficult and should fill countless gaming sessions.

## Calling in the Law

The Cast Members are laughed at should they attempt to tell civilized folks of the Blood Thing's existence. Kinatuk never allows its hordes to approach large groups of whites, at least not while there are so many of the monkeys left alive. Indians are different, however. They already believe in monsters and magic and so the Blood Thing is perfectly willing to send its hordes rampaging through their villages. Even better for Kinatuk, the traditional Indian loathing of dead things drives most of them off without fighting, leaving the old, weak and wounded to add to the monster's growing warband.

Most whites don't believe the heroes. Should an undead be captured and brought before the authorities, it simply plays dead—even allowing itself to be destroyed if need be. Kinatuk can be very clever when it needs to.

Isolated whites are a different matter. Lone trappers, mountain men, and distant farmers are perfect targets for the Blood Thing. It will not hesitate to add these humans to its collective essence. It can draw on some of their skills as well. A band of zombies with a few trappers and iron bear traps can make a nasty surprise for any band of heroes, even those with loads of True Grit.

A small locomotive filled with Kinatuk's undead is another nasty surprise. The "night train" pulls up to some lonesome town in the dark, allows passengers to climb on board and then adds them to its rolling larder. Stagecoaches and riverboats can serve this purpose as well.

## Complications

Once the secret of Kinatuk is revealed, the Zombie Master can liven up the campaign by throwing in a few of the following complications.

**General Goff:** The Cast Members are not the only ones who have found out about Kinatuk. General Ezekial "Blood and Guts" Goff is the new commander of the 7th Cavalry, based in newly built Fort Slaughter (named after one of Goff's associates, a Montana politician pushing for statehood). Recently, a Sioux warband was caught prowling around the Montana wilderness, far away from their reservation. Goff's standing orders are to shoot any Sioux caught off the reservation (Indian raids do not help a territory become a state, after all). One of the young men involved in the "raid," Heart of Bear, lived. He claimed the warband was attempting to destroy a great monster seen in a vision by his tribe's medicine man. Under "interrogation," the brave revealed the entire story of Kinatuk. Goff had the Indian executed and did not think any more of it for several weeks.

Then a patrol reported a strange encounter. While doing a routine check on one of the outlying farms, they came across a scene of carnage. The settlers lay strewn about their spread, mauled and bloody. The troopers dismounted and inspected the house—and the dead rose. The men fought their way out of the trap and returned to Fort Slaughter.

General Goff remembered Heart of Bear's words and quietly had one of his "henchman," Lieutenant Jonathan Douglass, check it out. Within two months, Douglass, Goff and a handpicked troop of the most ruthless men in the cavalry, knew the legend of the Blood Thing was real. Part of the legend, Goff also knew, involved capturing Kinatuk and harnessing its incredible power. Now he wants to capture Kinatuk alive and use it much like the ancient Anasazi once did.

Goff's special patrol—under Lieutenant Douglass—is now in hot pursuit of Kinatuk. They do not want the Blood Thing destroyed and the heroes' attempts to do just that undoubtedly lead to violence. Douglass, like his master and the handpicked men who serve him, is completely without morals. He'd sell his soul to the devil for the kind of power Kinatuk wields, so killing a few flies in the ointment does not bother him in the least. The lieutenant could even be an old rival of one of the Cast Members. Or perhaps he is a former Confederate known for slaughtering prisoners. If one of the heroes is a former slave, perhaps the lieutenant was his overseer long ago. The Zombie Master should personalize this villain so that his defeat can prove a significant milestone in vanquishing Kinatuk.

Soon after the party runs afoul of Lieutenant Douglass, Goff has false charges brought against them. The most likely charge is selling guns to the Indians. (This may be especially true if the heroes get involved in the next complication—The Warband.) Now the heroes face a real dilemma. The army is after them, meaning scores of good lawmen, soldiers, bounty hunters, and even common citizens are agin' them. Do they fight the "good guys" as well as the bad lieutenant? Or do they avoid shedding the blood of innocents and go after Kinatuk's zombies alone and with little chance of getting fresh supplies, ammunition, or even a doctor's care?

## Lieutenant Douglas

**Strength** 3     **Intelligence** 3

**Dexterity** 4     **Perception** 3

**Constitution** 3     **Willpower** 4

**Life Points** 46     **Speed** 14

**Endurance Points** 35     **Essence Pool** 20

**Qualities:** Acute Vision, Charisma +3, Fast as Hell, Fast Reaction Time, Hard to Kill 4, Nerves of Steel

**Drawbacks:** Cruel 2, Delusions (Murderous prejudice against Indians), Obsession (Personal power)

**Skills:** Brawling 1, Bureaucracy 2, Dancing (Formal) 1, Dodge 3, First Aid 2, Gambling 3, Guns (Handguns) 5, Guns (Rifle) 5, Hand Weapon (Saber) 5, Instruction 3, Intimidation 5, Questioning 3, Riding (Horse) 5, Stealth 2, Survival (Plains) 3, Tracking 2

**Gear:** Colt Dragoon with 24 Shells in Belt, Winchester '76 Rifle with 50 Shells, Saber

**The Warband:** Heart of Bear wasn't the only Sioux warrior chasing down Kinatuk. His medicine man, Sees Far, sent two bands of braves after the monstrous Blood Thing. The other band is led by White Stag, a fierce and difficult brute of a warrior with an intense hatred of white men. While he has a better chance of defeating the thing's hordes and eventually killing Kinatuk itself, his anger makes it especially difficult for White Stag to make allies in the white man's world.

The best way for the Zombie Master to introduce White Stag is to wait until late one night when the Cast Members are hip deep in the dead. They're about to be overwhelmed when White Stag and his band of eight other braves come wading into the fray like murderous ghosts, slashing and killing with reckless abandon. The Indians likely vanish into the night just as suddenly as they appear this first time.

## Typical Cavalryman

**Strength** 2     **Intelligence** 2

**Dexterity** 2     **Perception** 2

**Constitution** 3     **Willpower** 3

**Life Points** 30     **Speed** 10

**Endurance Points** 29     **Essence Pool** 14

**Skills:** Brawling 3, Dodge 2, First Aid 1, Gambling 1, Guns (Handgun) 2, Guns (Rifle) 3, Hand Weapon (Saber) 3, Intimidation 2, Notice 2, Riding (Horse) 4, Stealth 3, Survival (Plains) 2, Swimming 1, Tracking 1

**Gear:** Spencer Carbine with 50 Shells, Saber

The next time it happens, White Stag stays to issue a warning. "Leave this land, pale-faces! There are things here your murderous race cannot understand." The Zombie Master can let the party parlay from here, hopefully making a tenuous alliance over the destruction of Kinatuk. It may take White Stag months to give a grudging nod of approval to even the most selfless hero, but the rest of the warband should prove a little more open-minded (at least after a few battles against the undead together). The warband is also an excellent way to bring in new Indian Cast Members. Perhaps White Stag "assigns" them to the party to keep an eye on them and ensure they don't harm other Indians during their quest.

## White Stag

| | |
|---|---|
| **Strength** 4 | **Intelligence** 2 |
| **Dexterity** 3 | **Perception** 3 |
| **Constitution** 4 | **Willpower** 4 |
| **Life Points** 57 | **Speed** 14 |
| **Endurance Points** 41 | **Essence Pool** 20 |

**Qualities:** Fast Reaction Time, Good Luck 3, Hard to Kill 5, Nerves of Steel, Situational Awareness

**Drawbacks:** Cruel 1, Delusions (All white men are evil), Humorless, Minority, Obsession (Prove himself to his tribe), Showoff

**Skills:** Brawling 3, Climbing 2, Dodge 2, Guns (Handgun) 2, Hand Weapon (Tomahawk) 5, Intimidation 3, Myth and Legend (Sioux) 2, Notice 3, Occult Knowledge 1, Riding (Horse) 3, Stealth 5, Survival (Plains) 3, Swimming 2, Thrown 3, Tracking 4, Traps 2

**Gear:** Captured Spencer Carbine with 50 Shells, Tomahawk

## Typical Sioux Brave

| | |
|---|---|
| **Strength** 3 | **Intelligence** 2 |
| **Dexterity** 2 | **Perception** 2 |
| **Constitution** 3 | **Willpower** 2 |
| **Life Points** 34 | **Speed** 10 |
| **Endurance Points** 29 | **Essence Pool** 14 |

**Drawbacks:** Obsession (Prove himself to his tribe)

**Skills:** Brawling 2, Climbing 1, Dodge 3, Guns (Rifle) 2, Hand Weapon (Tomahawk) 3, Intimidation 2, Myth and Legend (Sioux) 1, Notice 2, Occult Knowledge 1, Riding (Horse) 3, Stealth 2, Survival (Plains) 3, Swimming 1, Thrown 3, Tracking 3

**Gear:** Captured Spencer Carbine with 10 Shells each, Tomahawk

# Grizzled Veteran
## Survivor

**Str** 4 **Dex** 3 **Con** 4
**Int** 2 **Per** 3 **Wil** 4
**LPs** 57
**EPs** 41
**Spd** 14
**Essence** 20

## Qualities/Drawbacks

Addiction (Alcohol) (-3)
    Cruel (-1)
      Emotional Problems
      (Stubborn) (-1)

Fast Reaction
Time (2)
Good Luck 3 (3)
Honorable (-3)
Hard to Kill 5 (5)
Resistance (Fatigue) (2)
Secret (ex-U.S. Marshal fired for
drunkenness) (-2)
True Grit (3)

## Skills

Brawling 3
Dodge 3
Gambling 3
Guns (Handgun) 4
Guns (Rifle) 4
Guns (Shotgun) 4
Hand weapon (Knife) 4
Intimidation 4
Notice 3
Riding (Horse) 4
Stealth 3
Survival (Plains) 3
Tracking 3

## Gear

Colt Peacemaker
with 24 Shells in Belt,
Winchester '76 Rifle
with 50 Shells

## Personality

Listen here, sister.  You asked for someone to take you to Fort Fetterman.  I did.  You asked me to quit drinkin' and swearin'.  I did that too.  Mostly.  When them Comanche chased us, I stayed back and fought 'em off, even though half my guts were fallin' out.  No special charge, just doin' my job.  Then you asked me to go inside with you and find out why the fort was deserted.  I did.  An' when that wounded sergeant tried to bite you, I blew his head off.  Never mind a feller can get hanged for shootin' a bluebelly—crazed or not.

An' now you want me to track this troop into Lakota territory.  Do you know what the Sioux do to white women?  It ain't mentionable.  Now I appreciate that you're the lieutenant's wife and all.  Maybe that'll get me outta trouble, maybe it won't.  But if those soldiers have crossed into the Nations, they're there to fight.  Your husband don't want no skirt chasin' him across the High Plains, and he sure as Hell don't want no drunken ex-Marshall escortin' her.

All right, stop yer sobbin'.  I'll help ya' find him.  But I don't believe in them visions o' yours.  There ain't no giant monster out there huntin' for your husband, lady.  And that sergeant I shot was just loco—not some kinda walkin'
— dead man.

## Quote

"Make one move and I'm gonna blow ya' durned head off."

# Tough Gal
## Survivor

**Str** 2 **Dex** 3 **Con** 3
**Int** 4 **Per** 4 **Wil** 4
**LPs** 45
**EPs** 32
**Spd** 12
**Essence** 20

## Qualities/Drawbacks

Acute Vision (2)
Attractiveness +2 (2)
Cruel (-1)
Fast as Hell (1)
Fast Reaction Time (2)
Hard to Kill 5 (5)
Honorable (-3)
Obsession (Proving she's as good as a man) (-2)
Reckless (-2)
Resistance (Pain) (3)
Showoff (-2)

## Skills

Brawling 3
Dodge 2
Guns (Handgun) 2
Guns (Rifle) 4
Guns (Shotgun) 5
Hand Weapon (Lasso) 3
Intimidation 2
Notice 3
Research/Investigation 2
Riding (Horse) 4
Smooth Talking 3
Stealth 3
Survival (Plains) 2
Swimming 2
Throwing 3
Tracking 2

## Gear

Winchester '76 Rifle with 50 Shells, Lasso

## Personality

You may not want me out here, Marshal, but you got me anyway. The lady said so. An' if you ask me, maybe you drink more, not less, 'cause you're denyin' what your own eyes and nose are tellin' you. That Injun wasn't rabid—he was dead! Just look at his mouth. That look normal to you?

Um, sure, I knowed rabid folks sometimes chewed their own lips. Shoot. Heh-heh. Ever-durned-fool knows that. What I meant to say was that, he, uh, he . . . well look at his blood! It's all black and rotten. And the stink. Smells like you wakin' up in your own chuck-up after a bender. Now I smelled plenty o' dead folks before. I scouted for Custer, if'n you recall, an' that Injun is dead. Twice, I reckon. I don't know how or why. Maybe it's some crazy Injun voodoo. Or maybe that lady's visions about some sorta monsters out here are true. But I do know I ain't afraid of 'em. If you had-n't plugged that varmint smack in the brainpan I'd'a done it myself. I just wanted to let you feel important, what with you only havin' one eye and all.

## Quote

"Yeehaa!"

# CHAPTER FIVE

# SPAGHETTI WITH MEAT

The wind whistled.

A swinging sign creaked in the breeze.

The hot sun loomed large over the abandoned town.

Stirrups shook on leather boots. Growing louder.

Flint drew a long match across his weathered holster. It flared loudly in the still heat.

The gunslinger lit his cigar, then looked up from under the brim of his hat. His cold, blue, narrow eyes winced from the sun as he looked down the street.

The dead were coming.

A cloud of dust rolled lazily in from the east. Flint could smell death inside. He heard air wheeze out of their bullet-ridden lungs. A hundred guns had already fallen to these dead men. Flint vowed he would not be one hundred and one.

The cloud settled. Three corpses stood with rotten hands on bony hips.

One out front, dressed in black, looked around the ghost town. "You're all alone, stranger." His voice sounded like a body dragged across gravel.

"I've got a friend here," Flint grunted and patted the Peacemaker on his hip.

"Ah. Mr. Colt. We know him well. Fickle bastard. Never know which side he's on."

Flint smiled. The dead had a sense of humor.

"I don't see a badge, stranger," said the dead man in black. "I can't imagine what they're payin' you. Enough for a nice casket, at least?"

"Or three."

The corpse in black cackled quietly. "You're even gonna taste funny."

Flint stopped smiling. That part was over. He reached slowly beneath his ratty poncho, then flipped something toward the corpse.

The dead man leaned down and picked up a badge, then slipped a rotten finger through the bullet-hole in its center. "Hmm. A law man who didn't get shot in the back. How unusual."

Flint's right eye twitched.

"Let me guess," the cadaverous gunslinger drawled with a voice like slowly breaking glass. "This was your brother. Or your father. Or your son. So many corpses, so little brain remaining. It's hard to remember. Was he family?"

"Family you're born with. Friends you choose. That was Hank Pilton. U.S. Marshal. Twice the man you are, alive or dead."

The undead gunslinger frowned. "Let's get this over with. I've places to go today."

Flint scowled. "Back to the grave, dead man. This time for good."

The thing stalled, looked back at his dead companions as if unsure. "Just what makes you think you got a chance, stranger?" His raspy voice wavered a bit at the end.

"You're afraid," Flint squared his jaw.

"Afraid? I'm not even alive, friend." The dead man tried to chuckle, but the air couldn't seem to break through his brittle throat.

"That so?" Flint reached up to his poncho and pulled it down a bit, revealing a white collar beneath his black shirt. "How you feel about that, Frank? Blessed the bullets in my gun myself."

"A preacher, huh? Killed a few of those, too." Despite the sneer on his face, Frank looked nervous.

Flint pressed his edge, stacking every possible advantage he could get. "I quit gunfighting a few years back. Hank Pilton was the man who taught me there were other ways. He coulda hung me. But he didn't. Now I owe him one. I figure makin' you a Swiss zombie oughtta do it."

Frank flinched, then went for his pistol. Flint was faster. He yanked his single-action Peacemaker and fanned the hammer four times. The first shot slammed into Frank's groin, the next three stitched up his gut and into his chin, bursting his skull like a rotten pumpkin.

The second corpse raised a shotgun, but Flint's next shot slipped into his heart before exploding out his spine from behind.

The last dead man's eyes grew wide in fear as he pulled two double-action Thunderers from their holsters. He managed one shot before Flint's final bullet took him in the pelvis and blew out his saddle-cushion. The zombie crumpled to the dirt, whimpering but still animate. Flint stepped slowly toward him, his spurs clinking with each ominous step.

"You'll never stop us . . ." the thing screeched. "We are only the beginning!"

"I'm the end," Flint said as he reloaded his six-gun.

## The Creaky Sign

A lone gunslinger stands in the street at High Noon. Music drifts in from the desert. A creaky sign sways in the wind. These are the elements of the "spaghetti western," named for the Italian-made films of the 1960s. By far the most famous of these were Clint Eastwood's "Man with No Name" series. Directed by Sergio Leone with music by Ennio Morricone, these films not only redefined the traditional John Wayne/John Ford westerns of the 1950s, but spawned a whole generation of knock-offs. Some of the imitators were even as good as Eastwood's films, most notably *Once Upon a Time in the West*, starring a young Charles Bronson.

The main feature of these films was their moody music, slow pace, and emphasis on style over complex plots and characterization. What does the viewer know of the protagonist? Very little. Sometimes the audience doesn't even know the hero's name. Rarely is anything known of his background. The viewer knows only that the main character is lightning with a six-gun. Though he is often gruff and unliked by "civilized" folks, it is he who they ultimately rely on to stand up to the true villains of the story. The "man with no name" is a dark loner, just short of a hero, just shy of a villain. A bad man who commits no evil on-screen—though one assumes his past is as shady as the dark side of a hanging tree.

These are the heroes of the spaghetti westerns. Only the undertaker smiles when these veterans enter the Deadworld of Spaghetti with Meat.

## Men with No Names

Cast Members in Spaghetti with Meat should be tough loners looking to make a few bucks, or perhaps even drifters hiding out from the law in the backwaters of the High Plains. Shady is the key word here.

Getting a pack of loners like these to work together can be a bit tough. *The Outlaw Josey Wales* would not have been as suspenseful with a band of four other gunslingers backing the protagonist all the time. For those who have seen that film, though, it's worth remembering that Wales became an outlaw only after a crooked Union officer gunned down his surrendered Confederate company. Even then, he picked up two Indian sidekicks (one of whom, a woman, decided she was "married" to him). In other films, Eastwood's drifter sided with gunmen of a different breed, like Lee Van Cleef in the Man with No Name trilogy. One of the tricks to making the party composition feel right is to make sure everyone isn't a squinty-eyed, cigar-chewing gunslinger with a poncho and a slouch hat. Perhaps one of the heroes is a well-dressed gunman from Back East (like Van Cleef's character). Another might be a young Billy the Kid type looking to prove his speed with a six-gun. Still another might be a whimsical drifter like Charles Bronson's harmonica-playing hero from *Once Upon a Time in the West*. Indians are also appropriate, though most tend to be the older and wiser variety. Knife-wielding braves don't last long here, but a pissed-off half-breed with a Winchester fits right in. Preachers and nuns offer another character type, particularly as their connection to the Almighty might just stave off a zombie attack.

## Recommended Qualities and Drawbacks

Any gunslinger worth her salt ought to have the Fast as Hell Quality.

Fast Reaction Time is also critical as lone hombres with bad attitudes tend to be outnumbered in their all-too frequent gun-fights.

Situational Awareness also comes in handy when the bad guys realize they can't take a gunslinger in a fair fight and decide to bushwhack her from behind instead.

As for Drawbacks, characters with Secrets and shady pasts often have Adversaries who hunt for them. Hired guns with bad reputations (deserved or not) might have negative Status as well.

## Once Upon a Time in the West

Spaghetti with Meat is set during the latter part of the Civil War. Anytime between 1864 and 1865 works best. This is a great time for the good, the bad, and the ugly, as old rivalries and war wounds fester in the Texas heat. A Yankee caught alone in Texas had best go heeled and a Southerner in Dodge City had best not cross paths with the former Union Marshal. The nation is at war and her children are bleeding.

## The Quick and the Dead

The dead in Spaghetti with Meat arose from the works of one corrupt shyster, a traveling snake-oil salesman named Alouicious Rheems. That's "Al-oo-wish-us" for those tinhorns from Back East who have never seen the name before.

Alouicious trailed the Northern and Southern armies selling his wares to desperate and dying soldiers looking for anything to save their lives. The snake oil did nothing, of course, but Rheems got used to spending the money on women, wine and cigars. Then he got caught and nearly hanged. Through sheer dumb luck, he managed to escape and decided a change of scenery was in order.

He turned to the West, figuring the ongoing violence there would bring him a brand new clientele. He enjoyed some success, but robbing soon-to-be widows and orphans wasn't nearly as profitable as taking the money of dying soldiers. One dark night, Alouicious made a deal. He asked the devil to make his potion work—"to bring peace to the wounded and give life to the dead." It was a poor choice of words.

Lucifer was listening. The next night, Rheems' potion did just what he'd asked.

An outlaw named Pete "Scratch" Wilson and his gang, the Texas Devils, caught up with Alouicious riding the Chisholm Trail. Scratch, named for the Devil himself, and his gang had been shot up bad robbing the Dodge City bank. The bandits demanded that Rheems pull over his wagon and when they saw what he carried, decided to give it a try. Scratch thought the snake oil was probably nothing more than rotgut whiskey with a few extras thrown in, but figured that would at least relieve the pain of the gruesome gutshot he was trying to hide from the rest of his cutthroats. He gave the stuff a swig and almost instantly felt better.

"Drink up, boys!" Scratch yelled, handing out cases of Rheems' Miracle Elixir to his gang. Over thirty of the bloodiest bandits in the Southwest drank Rheems' tonic. They whooped, hollered and fired their guns in celebration. This was truly magical—those with the worst wounds proved it.

Exactly one hour later, as the bandits lay scattered around the busted bottles and ruined crates, the fire set in. Each man felt it start in his stomach—a hot sensation like he'd eaten four-alarm Texas chili. Then it spread to their loins, their throats, their extremities, and finally their brains. The outlaws screamed. Scratch himself pulled his pistol and shot Rheems straight through the brainpan.

Some of the bandits—angry, ignorant men from the start—fired on each other. The gang knew they were dying. An agonizing ten minutes later, the High Plains were quiet once again.

The bodies lay in the hot sun all day. A few predators, coyotes, gophers, a buzzard, and even a lost cat nibbled on the Devils' rotting remains. As darkness fell, the scavengers withdrew, sensing something tainted and unclean stirring up from within the decaying meat. When a full moon rose over the prairie and the clock struck midnight, Scratch Wilson rose from the ground with a scream dragged straight from the pits of Hell. In moments, his gang joined him, risen dead hungry for meat.

The gang shared Rheems' corpse, then hunted for game and ate that raw too. Their horses would have nothing to do with them, so they shot them and fed them Rheems' tonic as well. The animals quickly rose to serve their masters once again.

Slowly, Scratch and the others realized what a boon these new undead forms were. They were practically unkillable. If they played their cards right, they could go on a crime spree the likes of which had never been known before. And no town full of trigger-happy part-time lawmen could stop them.

The undead gunmen split into several smaller groups. Each one of these new gangs is captained by one of Scratch's original companions. Scratch himself remains in the outlands, allowing his captains to operate on their own and return to their camp once in a while to share their wealth. To end the zombie threat in this adventure, the Cast Members must track down Scratch. He has the remaining wagon-load of Rheems' brew, which he uses periodically to make more zombie banditos. If Scratch can be killed—again—and the elixir destroyed, the Cast Members can then track down the last of the outlaws and end this scourge forever.

## The Undead

Scratch Wilson and his original bandits are far more powerful than later batches—Scratch diluted the elixir with a little whiskey to make it go farther. Scratch and his gang take no damage from normal weapons, but can be slain with objects blessed by a holy man. Also, blessed objects cause double damage. A priest who finds out about Scratch might suggest this. Later batches of the undead can be killed by anything—as long as the brain is targeted. All of the zombies retain the memories and personalities of life and a little more of their skills than is usual for zombies, as is reflected in their skill list. This will vary their power level by one point per skill level. The gang has Colt Walkers with 48 rounds each (some have shotguns and rifles as well), large knives, and undead horses. Scratch holds all the magical elixir and always has "just enough for a few more."

## Three Amigos

The story opens with the heroes in a saloon in the south Texas town of Cerbeza. Each player should figure out for herself what her character is doing there. One might be after a bounty, another may simply be there for a long, tall drink. Still another might be engaged in a high-stakes poker game—or desperately trying to win enough dinero for her next meal.

The action starts around dusk. Three tough-looking hombres enter the saloon and head straight for the bar. They order a bottle of the cheapest rotgut and

## Scratch Wilson and the First Batch

**Strength** 2    **Intelligence** 2

**Dexterity** 2    **Perception** 1

**Constitution** 2    **Willpower** 2

**Dead Points** 26    **Speed** 4

**Endurance Points** n/a    **Essence Pool** 11

**Attack:** By weapon type; Scratch has a Guns (Handgun, Rifle, Shotgun) 5 and Hand Weapon (Knife) 3; his original gang all have Guns (Handgun, Rifle, Shotgun) 4 and Hand Weapon (Knife) 3

**Weak Spot:** None (10), Blessed Objects (-5)

**Getting Around:** Life-Like (3)

**Strength:** Dead Joe Average (0)

**Senses:** Like the Living (1), Scent Tracking (1)

**Sustenance:** Occasionally (2), All Flesh Must Be Eaten (0)

**Intelligence:** Language (1), Long-Term Memory (5), Problem Solving (15), Teamwork (4)

**Spreading the Love:** Special (Elixir, -2)

**Power:** 57 (Scratch), 54 (others)

## Later Batches

**Strength** 2    **Intelligence** 2

**Dexterity** 2    **Perception** 1

**Constitution** 2    **Willpower** 2

**Dead Points** 15    **Speed** 4

**Endurance Points** n/a    **Essence Pool** 11

**Attack:** By weapon type, zombie banditos have a skill 2 in any weapon type required

**Weak Spot:** Brain (6)

**Getting Around:** Life-Like (3)

**Strength:** Dead Joe Average (0)

**Senses:** Like the Living (1); Scent Tracking (1)

**Sustenance:** Occasionally (2); All Flesh Must Be Eaten (0)

**Intelligence:** Language (1), Long-Term Memory (5), Problem Solving (15), Teamwork (4)

**Spreading the Love:** None (-4)

**Power:** 51

start drinking the stuff like water—literally. These are three of the Devils' most recent recruits—Mexican banditos they ran into just over the border. The three freshly dead men are just getting used to their new state and have discovered that alcohol, in copious amounts, can effectively pickle them and turn their stench down a notch or two. Wilson has ordered everyone to stay away from civilized areas, but discipline among outlaws is less than stellar.

If someone picks a fight with the Mexicans—two brothers named Juan and Manuel and their friend Jose—are quick to respond. They know they can't be killed and are eager to test out their new powers in a gunfight. If no one starts trouble with them, they head for the nearest soiled doves and begin to paw at the girls roughly. The ladies—sensing something isn't right about these men—refuse, and the three amigos get even rougher. Most likely, someone in the party gets involved. If not, one of the ladies pushes Manuel away and he stumbles backward, upending one of the Cast Members' tables and sending whiskey, cards and poker chips flying. If the gunslinging heroes do not get involved after this, they aren't ornery enough. Perhaps a direct appeal from one of the ladies might rouse them to action, particularly if one of the three amigos is dragging her violently out into the back alley or an upstairs room.

The gunfight with the three amigos should be relatively short and bloody. The rest of the bar's patrons duck for cover, leaving Juan, Manuel, and Jose to trade shots with the heroes. This is a great time to try out the showdown rules (see p. 33). Of course, shots to any area but the brain do not hurt the amigos much, but when they realize they are outgunned, they crash through the window in typical Western style and attempt to escape on their nervous (but not undead) horses tied up outside. Any who were shot and killed in the saloon stay that way and do not prove a thing to the "witnesses." Should a hero claim one of the amigos was already dead, the locals simply look at the corpse and exchange nervous glances with one another about this "loco" stranger who thinks the dead walk.

If no one pursues the escaped bandits, they hightail it into the local badlands and hide out there until the next encounter. If pursued, the Cast Members likely learn the valuable lesson of just how to kill these undead banditos. Unlike most zombies, the dead in Spaghetti with Meat do actually care if they continue to exist. Torture has no effect on the unfeeling dead, but a very real threat to paint the desert floor with their brains elicits a more positive response. Should one of the banditos be captured in some way, he reveals only that he was shot but brought back to life by some sort of foul-tasting green elixir administered by a gang called the Devils. He's now part of the gang, and the boss, who he calls Scratch, is planning a big job very soon. The zombie does not know what the target is (Wilson has not told him) and he does not know where it is, but he knows the attack is happening within the next few days. He has seen at least a dozen members of the gang, but there may well have been more in other campsites. The zombie can lead the heroes to where the Devils were supposed to be, but they have moved on now, leaving only a cold campfire and a couple of bony steer carcasses. An Intelligence and Tracking Task reveals there are about a dozen in this group (which is only part of the larger gang—they scatter to avoid capture by any pursuing authorities). Of course, the survivor speaks only Spanish (Mexican, actually), so a party without a translator gets very little out of the corpse but "No speakada Englaiz."

## Cerbeza, Texas

Back in Cerbeza, Research and/or Streetwise Tasks reveal there is nothing here the bandits could possibly be after. Even the bank is a very small affair with perhaps a couple of hundred dollars stored in its safe on the busiest day. And as far as anyone knows, there are no other big targets for bandits within a hundred miles. To string things out a bit, the Zombie Master can throw in rumors of other possible sites—silver strikes in the desert, larger banks or trains coming through with valuable cargo. These red herrings can lead to plenty of interesting subplots and give the players a chance to further define their characters' personalities. It's also possible that other gangs or bandits make a play for one of these prizes, giving the heroes a few more chances to slap leather. It might even turn out that some of these bandits are those who will help Wilson and the Devils later on.

This might give the Cast Members some additional clues about the villains, as well as making the battle more personal.

Cerbeza is home to about 40 citizens. Another 200 or so live within a 25-mile radius (though few if any of these feel any ties or loyalty to the community). The town serves as a supply point for these settlers—mostly ranchers—and as a hiring point for ranch and trail hands who come for the annual cattle drives. Most of the beeves (cattle) in this neck of Texas are earmarked for the war effort Back East.

Folks here have mixed attitudes about the War of Secession (as most Southerners call it). Those who have sent sons or fathers are adamant about the cause. They do not tolerate Northerners and the most violent and ignorant might just draw down on someone for having the wrong accent (or lack thereof). Most folks, however, could care less about the war. It is a long way away and the Mexicans are seen as a much greater danger than a watchful Federal government.

Cerbeza is home to four simple businesses, the Town Hall, and around two-dozen homes. Since Cerbeza serves as the starting point for this setting, some more detail on these establishments is in order. The Zombie Master should feel free to add additional details, characters, and subplots to the town as needed. A map of the town is included on p. 92.

## Dead Dog Saloon

The Dead Dog is the town's most popular watering hole. It has rotgut whiskey, strong beer brewed by a local German, and even a bottle or two of wine for special occasions. The owner, Max Stengle, is from Alabama and fought in the war for the first few months until he lost an arm at 1st Manassas (1st Bull Run to Yankees). Suffering such a loss in the very first battle of the war made Max more bitter toward Yankees and the North than most. He will not serve a Yankee and even expels them given the slightest provocation. That said, Max is not eager to get shot. Should a character push Max, he quietly serves up some drinks and does not say another word until night. Then he talks some of the town's worst troublemakers into provoking the cowboy into an unfair fight. If things are really bad, Max is not above

shooting someone in the back as they stagger to their room at night.

The Dead Dog has nine round tables with room for five to six customers each. Bar stools hold another eight patrons. It opens around lunch time (noon) and closes no earlier than 2 am. Besides Max, two serving girls, Ellie May and Maria Alonzo, work the tables and cook the food. Both girls are single, though some of the locals may claim them as their girlfriends should any strangers get too familiar with them.

At any given time, there are 2D10 + 5 customers inside, eating, drinking, playing poker, or just sitting (there is really nowhere else to go). When the three Confederates arrive (see p. 93), they spend the entire afternoon in the Dead Dog.

## Davis' General Store

Martha Davis is the war-bride of John C. Davis, now a colonel in Sam Hood's Texas Brigade (serving in Lee's Army of Northern Virginia). Her two young sons fight under their father, though at least one of them has been lost and assumed dead for several months now. She's a proud, feisty woman in her late fifties. She flies the rebel flag proudly and while she's a devout believer in states' rights and the Confederate cause, she isn't as hostile to Yankees as one might believe. Martha thinks war was one step too far and actually blames Southern hotheads as much as Yankee "aggression" for her family's fate. She's smart enough not to tell any of the locals her feelings, however.

Her store has all the necessities, clean and properly organized. Her prices are fair and she often quietly extends credit to those in need. If the heroes cause trouble in town and are not clearly justified, Martha does not sell them bullets or firearms. She does not want to see her town torn apart by trigger-happy drifters and is not afraid to say so. She keeps a loaded double-barreled shotgun under the counter and she knows how to use it.

Martha also runs a small boarding house. With her family gone, she has moved their things out and rents the rooms for one dollar a night, meals included. She keeps a strict house. A customer who causes trouble in town finds his things packed out on the front

Spaghetti with Meat

porch. On the flip side, if Martha feels a character is getting a raw deal, she may quietly help him out.

## Farmer's Bank of Texas

Cerbeza's bank is small, catering mostly to the ranchers while they're away on long drives to Kansas. Even these folks deposit only a small portion of their funds into the bank. Like most folks in the West, they do not trust banks or bankers, and even those they do trust are eventually robbed anyway. Besides, no interest rates on deposits means the Mason jar out back is a safer place to store the family's money than some stranger's safe. Should what's in the bank's safe become an issue, call it 5D10 x $100 in cash and another D10 x $100 in jewelry.

The owner of the bank is Fred Turnbull. Despite the neighbors' predilection to mistrust bankers, he is actually a very honest man. He and his family live in town and are genuinely interested in making it a peaceful (and profitable) place to live. His daughter, Nell, is now 20 years old and most of the young bucks in town are eager for her hand and daddy's (mostly perceived) fortune. Should the heroes make much trouble, Fred is one of the first to offer a quiet bounty on their heads. Nell, however, has a thing for "bad boys." If she gets caught with a rough-and-tumble gunslinger, Fred is even more likely to offer up a bounty.

## Stable and Livery

Franz Mueller never named his livery, he just put up a barn and started charging people to stable, shoe, and groom their horses. Most days his stable is empty, so Franz spends his time making strong German beer and selling it to Max Stengle at the Dead Dog saloon and whatever locals wander in for a few quarts. Franz is a typical German—thick gray "chops," a strong back and a thick accent. A lot of folks in town just call him "the German." Franz has a son fighting for the Union, but the only person in the state who knows it is Martha Davis. Like most Germans in the period, he has a soft spot for Yankees and might be a source of potential help for bluebellies who run afoul of Max Stengle or the rest of the

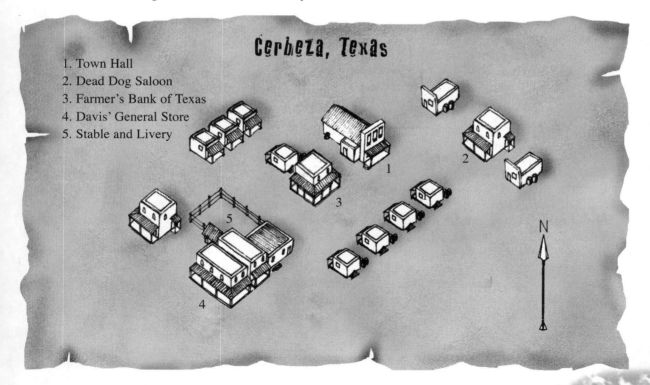

Cerbeza, Texas

1. Town Hall
2. Dead Dog Saloon
3. Farmer's Bank of Texas
4. Davis' General Store
5. Stable and Livery

town. (As a rule, Germans were known to support the Federal cause. The townsfolk do not think much of it, but the Zombie Master might point it out to any Cast Members with strong allegiances as an additional subplot.)

## Town Hall

Town Hall serves as a meeting place for the local council, claims office, notary, jail, and even a makeshift church before the local preacher went off to serve the cause. The Town Marshal, Whitey Ford, can be found here most days, reading whatever newspaper he can get from Dallas, Tombstone, or wherever the last traveler came from. There are no other occupants here unless the town council calls a meeting. Whitey has no deputies. Whitey keeps a couple of shotguns and a rifle in a locked cabinet in his office should real trouble arise—which it never has.

## Trouble Comes in Threes

The Zombie Master should trigger the next event when the party gets restless. At that point, three Confederate soldiers enter town. The heroes do not know it yet, but these men are deserters from the Confederate Army. They raided a bank in Missouri two years back and hid the loot in one of the rebels' hometowns—Cerbeza. It is buried in the grave of Ernest Mullins, a private. He was killed at Shiloh last year. His "friends" claimed his body was too "ripped up by Yankee canister" for public viewing and buried him with a closed casket in Cerbeza's "boot hill." In truth, Mullins' body still lies on the field of Shiloh. In his coffin is nearly $40,000 worth of loot, most of which is gold.

The three men were at Vicksburg when it surrendered but slipped out of the city just before they were to lay down their arms. Now the three have returned to Cerbeza to unearth the casket and claim their ill-gotten gold. What they do not know is that the fifth member of their band, mortally wounded at Champion Hill (fought before Vicksburg), slipped into a delirium while in hospital. There he was bedded beside one of Scratch Wilson's companions and

revealed the secret of the stolen gold. Wilson does not know exactly where the gold is—the dying rebel just said it was "buried somewhere in Cerbeza." Wilson figures on riding into town, killing everyone in it and then taking his time digging up the gold. Cerbeza is a small town, but killing over two hundred civilians is a bit risky, even for a band of zombies. So Scratch is taking his time, recruiting more scum and planning a bloody raid that will make the atrocities of the Civil War look like a tussle in a kindergarten sandbox.

The three remaining Confederate thieves are John Dingle, Lawrence Mobley, and Hank Ingersoll. John and Lawrence are from Alabama; Hank is a native Texan and knew the deceased Ernest Mullins before the war (though Hank is from El Paso, not Cerbeza). They enter town around high noon, then plan on drinking and having dinner at the Dead Dog until nightfall. Around midnight, they will rendezvous at the graveyard, dig up the casket, and ride out of town that night. Max Stengle at the Dead Dog and Martha Davis both remember the men as the ones who brought Ernest Mullins' body home. The men do not speak to them much, however, despite being quite friendly when they visited previously.

The heroes might realize something is odd about the three men if they see them ride into town. Besides their change of demeanor from their previous visit, each man has a brand new shovel strapped to his saddle. One of them has a coat draped over the shovel, but the other two are plainly evident. If asked separately, the men give conflicting stories. If asked as a group, Dingle says their company issued them to everyone to help rebuild earthworks. They are on leave now and just packed all their gear with them (though they have no muskets). Anyone who asks too many questions chases the men off—they then plan on coming back later that night when there are not so many nosy types around. The three thieves are not keen on a gunfight—they are close to being wealthy and would now rather die with their boots off. Still, if pressed, the hot-blooded Southerners may well slap leather.

## Confederate Thieves

**Strength** 2  **Intelligence** 2
**Dexterity** 3  **Perception** 2
**Constitution** 3  **Willpower** 2
**Life Points** 39  **Speed** 12
**Endurance Points** 26  **Essence Pool** 14

**Qualities:** Fast Reaction Time, Hard to Kill 3

**Drawbacks:** Covetous (Greedy) 3, Secret (Deserters)

**Skills:** Brawling 2, Dodge 2, Guns (Handgun) 4, Guns (Musket) 4, Guns (Shotgun) 4, Hand Weapon (Knife) 3, Intimidation 3, Notice 2, Riding (Horse) 3, Stealth 2, Survival (Desert) 2, Throwing 2, Tracking 2

**Gear:** Single-action Colt Walker Pistols with 24 Shots, Shovel, Horse

## The Probe

The night the three rebels arrive, around 11 am, the Devils raid. Fortunately for the locals, this is just a scouting mission. Scratch has convinced a band of a dozen human banditos to "hurrah" the town. They are to simply ride up and down the street, break a few windows with their pistolas, and shoot anyone who gives them even the slightest excuse. Should a posse pursue, his men are ready to ambush and wipe them out, leaving that many less defenders for the real attack later on.

Wilson himself does not take part in either fight. He is on a hilltop a few hundred yards away with a spyglass to see whether the town fights back or scatters. He also wants to see who in town deserves

"special" attention. Should the heroes distinguish themselves, he takes special care to deal with them himself during the real attack.

During the fight, one of the three Confederate thieves finds himself caught out in the street during the bandits' rush. The thief fights back and kills at least one of the banditos, proving that he is a fighter and perhaps giving the heroes a reason to recruit him in the next scene.

In the end, it does not really matter how successful the bandits are. At least one of them, however (perhaps the one shot by the Confederate), is wounded and can be questioned. All he knows is that some smelly white man paid him and his crew to hurrah the town. He has no idea why. The man who hired him calls himself the Devil and smells like he has bathed in rotten tequila (Scratch uses the alcohol to disguise his decaying stench).

If the party does not realize what's going on, there are two ways for the Zombie Master to clue them in. The first is to let them see a glint of light from Wilson's spyglass. They do not find him if they rush the ridge he was hiding on, but they at least realize someone is watching. Anyone with any military background should instantly realize this is a probe. A second way to clue the heroes in is to have one of the three Confederate thieves make the same guess a little too loudly.

## The Magnificent Seven

The heroes might now be aware that a large attack is coming. They do not know when or by whom, but it is definitely coming. This is where survival horror comes back into the picture. The Devils are intent on destroying the entire town and everyone in it. They cannot let anyone escape because they might return with the Texas Rangers or other authorities. That would not only jeopardize the gold but would likely reveal the existence of the undead to them as well. And Scratch sure as hell does not want that.

Exactly what happens next depends on the party's actions.

**High Plains Drifter:** If the Cast Members go to the local law, they find Town Marshal Whitey Ford.

Although he is not much with a gun anymore, every Success Level on a Smooth Talking Task gets him to round up one of the town's nineteen able-bodied men to help (most are off fighting the war). If the heroes assume command (Whitey is not eager to do it himself), they can place the posse wherever they want in anticipation of the ambush. The map of Cerbeza is provided for both the Zombie Master and the players (see p. 92). The heroes should be allowed to use it to plot out the town's defense.

If the heroes know who's coming, they might set a few psychological traps as well. In the film *High Plains Drifter*, the Man with No Name painted the town red and put up a sign that said "Welcome to Hell." The bandits set to attack the town (as in this scenario) were quite unsettled when they saw they were riding into a trap. Scratch is not put out by intimidation tactics, but his minions might if the Zombie Master is impressed by the Cast Members' actions.

The three Confederate thieves refuse to join in any plan. They just want to get their gold and get out. They could care less about Cerbeza. A ruthless party might get them to reveal their plans—quietly—if they somehow force every able-bodied man into service. Should that happen, the rebels promise to give the heroes a third (no more), if they can have the rest and get out of town.

If the Confederates' plan is not discovered, they may lie and promise to help to get the heroes off their backs. They then desert the group at the worst possible moment to go dig up the gold. Should this happen, the Zombie Master should contrive a way for the three to be caught, killed, and recruited by Scratch, adding three more competent gunmen to his band.

**Playing it Cool:** If the Cast Members decide to play it cool and just wait to see what happens, that's fine too. It just makes it that much harder to survive when the Devils strike. The three Confederate thieves desert at the worst possible time in this scenario as well. Perhaps they are watching the heroes' backs when they decide to make a break for the graveyard and the gold. If they are stopped, one of them tells the heroes their secret with his dying breath. If they are not stopped, they go to the graveyard and are shot as above.

# Welcome to Hell

In either case, the Devils strike at midnight. Wilson sends any surviving bandits (twelve plus however many survived the day raid) in first. The first six have torches and throw them into the saloon, the hotel and the general store. The rest shoot anyone they see. Men, women and children are all targets (though a few of the human bandits may look the other way if a woman or a child crosses their path). Wilson has already sent those who objected to the slaughter to Lucifer.

The zombies ride into town next. There are seventeen of these including Scratch Wilson. The bandit chief cannot afford to let anyone escape, so he presses relentlessly. He is a bad, bad man, so no tactic is beneath him. If the heroes hole up in a building, he burns it down. If they run, he chases them. He might also use captured townsfolk as "bait" to lure the Cast Members out (where he plans on shooting them all). The Zombie Master should feel free to be as dirty and as graphic as the group can handle. This is a spaghetti western, after all. The good guys are not saints— so the bad guys are downright evil, greedy, dirty, and mean. If Scratch cannot just kill the heroes, he will not seriously endanger himself.

If this game is a one-shot, the Zombie Master can end it with the heroes' deaths, a grim showdown with Scratch in the middle of the fight or a cat-and-mouse killing game in the town's shadows.

If this game is part of a campaign, Scratch runs off with the wagon carrying the last few cases of elixir to make a new gang. The heroes must now pursue him and his minions across the West, all the while dodging the undead assassins, gunslingers, and lawmen Scratch "converts" to the dead side.

A particularly interesting finale to the battle in town might end with Max Stengle bringing the heroes a few bottles of his best. He apologizes for anything he said before and toasts to their victory over the "horrors from the desert." The heroes drink up and notice Max smiling. Slowly, they realize they've just drunk Scratch's elixir . . .

*Spaghetti with Meat*

# The Drifter
## Survivor

**Str** 3 **Dex** 5 **Con** 3
**Int** 3 **Per** 3 **Wil** 3
**LPs** 46
**EPs** 32
**Spd** 16
**Essence** 20

## Qualities/Drawbacks

Acute Senses (2)
Addiction (Cigars) (-1)
Adversary (Wanted in several
territories) (-3)
Fast as Hell (1)
Fast Reaction Time (2)
Good Luck 3 (3)
Hard to Kill 4 (4)
Lazy (-2)
Nerves of Steel (3)
Recurring Nightmares (-1)
Secret (Wanted in several
territories) (-3)

## Skills

Brawling 4
Demolitions 3
Dodge 4
Guns (Handgun) 5
Guns (Rifle) 2
Guns (Shotgun) 3
Intimidation 5
Notice 3
Riding (Horse) 4
Stealth 3
Survival (Desert) 3
Throwing 2
Tracking 2
Swimming 2

## Gear

Single-action Colt
Peacemaker with 24
Shots, Fast-draw
Holster, Serape (cloth pon-
cho)

## Personality

There's a price on your head, amigo. You know what that means?

That's right. I'm gonna take you in. We can do it the hard way, or the easy way. The hard way is alive. The easy way is I shoot you through the heart and throw you on the back of my horse. Trouble is, my horse eats meat. Damnest thing I ever saw, but ol' Gunsmoke rides good. Thing is, he might nibble your face off when I stop for the night. You got no face, I get no reward. So I pre- fer the hard way.

It's your choice, amigo. Drop your pistola and put on those manacles, or skin that smokewagon and let's see if Gunsmoke likes Mexican.

## Quote

None—just a quiet, twitching-eye stare.

# Bad Girl
## Survivor

**Str** 3 **Dex** 3 **Con** 3
**Int** 3 **Per** 4 **Wil** 4
**LPS** 49
**EPS** 35
**Spd** 12
**Essence** 20

## Qualities/Drawbacks

Acute Vision (2)
Attractiveness +2 (2)
Cruel (-1)
Delusion (Prejudice against Indians) (-3)
Delusion (Prejudice against Mexicans) (-3)
Fast as Hell (1)
Fast Reaction Time (2)
Hard to Kill 5 (5)
Minority (Aggressive woman) (-1)
Nerves of Steel (3)
Obsession (Be tough as
any hombre) (-2)

## Skills

Brawling 3
Cheating 2
Dodge 2
Guns (Handgun) 4
Guns (Rifle) 4
Guns (Shotgun) 5
Intimidation 4
Notice 4
Occult Knowledge 1
Research/Investigation 2
Riding (Horse) 3
Stealth 3
Streetwise 3
Swimming 2
Tracking 3

## Gear

Shotgun with 12
Shells, Rough
Pants and Shirt

## Personality

You can snigger all you want, but remember I spent some time with the Shawnee 'afore I got traded to Mexicans. It wasn't a pleasant time, and I've killed more n' my fair share o' both for what they did, but the Injuns showed me things white folks ain't never heard of. Things you wouldn't believe. That dirty bandito we just filled full o' lead wasn't cranked up on peyote—he was dead.

Don't you laugh at me! Especially you, senorita! I'll shove this sawed-off right up your baby-maker and decorate the casa with your cabesa-beans!"

That's better. Now I didn't come south o' the border 'cause I wanted to. An' I didn't come in this cantina to drink dirty Mexican piss-water. I came here 'cause them bandits you're trackin' got a high bounty, an' I don't think you nor any other Army-reject is gonna know how to kill 'em. I do. Least I do now. Now are we partners?

Or should I just keep my secrets to myself?

### Quote

"The only good bandito's a dead bandito."

97

# CHAPTER SIX

# DANCES WITH ZOMBIES

General George Armstrong Custer looked out across the Big Horn and frowned. There were more teepees in the winding river valley than he had expected. Worse, like Sand Creek, the braves wouldn't fight. They'd run off and leave their women and children at the mercy of their enemies. Just didn't make sense to Custer's way of thinking, but he'd learned long ago that the red man was more than a little strange and barbaric . . . not to mention cowardly. The Indians might kill innocent home-steaders and their families; Custer detested killing women and children, despite what the papers Back East said.

"I want the braves, Tom," he said to his brother. "I don't care to cart a wagon full of children back to General Crook."

"Just how you plan to do that? You know they'll just run off like always." His brother had been hunting Indian troublemakers by his side for a long time. He knew as much, if not more about the red man's ways.

Custer nodded and stroked his yellow beard. "We'll send Reno to hurrah the camp with one bat-talion. We'll take the rest of the regiment and circle round the far side to cut off their escape. Keep Benteen in reserve."

"You want the Gatlings brought up?" They'd been assigned several of the new-fangled repeating guns but they were clumsy things and difficulty to move about.

"No, there'll be no place for 'em. This will be a running fight. They seem to have plenty of good horses down there."

"All right." Good old Tom, couldn't find a better man to have at your side when the shooting start-ed. Not that this would be much of a fight though. Maybe they could catch the fleeing braves and put an end to this trouble here and now. The Indians weren't great thinkers; they had to slip up at some point. General Custer planned to be there when that happened.

"Get me Reno."

\* \* \*

Sitting Bull looked down at the bloody mess at his feet. United States soldiers, dressed in blue, lay all around. He had dreamed this. He had dreamed of defeating Custer and the entire white man's army. Though he had told no one, he had also dreamed of destroying the white man's race. And he knew how to make his dream become real. Little magic was left in the world—it faded with his dying people—but there was enough for one last curse.

Crazy Horse approached, his hands, face, and chest covered in blood—white man's blood. "This is Yellow Hair?"

Sitting Bull nodded.

Crazy Horse knelt and drew his long knife.

"No," Sitting Bull placed a hand on his greatest brave's shoulder. "I have something else in mind."

## Indian Games

In this setting, the Cast Members are all Indians of the Sioux tribe, shortly after the massacre of the 7th Cavalry Regiment at the Battle of the Little Bighorn in June 1876.

Relations between the Sioux and the encroaching whites were at an all-time low prior to Custer's famous Last Stand. The Sioux claimed the Black Hills (Pa Sapa) as their own, though Crow Indians claimed them as well (and they had taken them from the Cheyenne years before). When gold was discovered there, the government (urged by Custer himself) declared the area off-limits to whites. Squatters literally invaded the region, however, and soon violence erupted between stalking Indians and heavily-armed miners. Eventually, the government decided to move the Indians out of the Black Hills and scatter the tribes into new, smaller lands.

Sitting Bull and others of the "Sioux Nations" called in as many of the Sioux and allied tribes as possible to resist.

Three columns of United States soldiers, including infantry, cavalry, and even artillery, struck out into the Dakotas, Montana, and Wyoming east of the Black Hills to disrupt the "hostiles" and forcibly remove them to their new reservations.

The columns encountered light resistance, then fought two substantial engagements before Custer's group found the Sioux camp. An experienced Indian fighter, Custer was far more afraid that the Indian warriors would mount up and escape than he was about them putting up serious resistance. Though the brash cavalryman knew many of the Indians were actually better armed than his own troops, the Sioux rarely stood to fight against regular soldiers. Life was precious to the small tribes. Losing braves meant the inability to protect the tribe from enemies (including other Indians) and

Dances with Zombies

more importantly, no one to hunt for buffalo and other game. Thus the Sioux often retreated from stand-up battles and preferred to raid isolated groups of whites instead. Unfortunately for the Sioux, they saw little difference between a white family of farmers and the blue-clad soldiers who chased them. This poisoned frontier whites against them and made aggression against the natives all-too justifiable. Thus the political climate for a war against the Sioux was generated, and the 7th Cavalry was one of the weapons the government would fight it with.

Though General Alfred Terry was in command of the column, Custer commanded the 7th Cavalry regiment and was the first to contact the Sioux. At the Little Bighorn, Custer split his command into three groups. One was led by Custer himself. The flamboyant "Yellow Hair" was officially a Lieutenant Colonel, but he had been "brevetted" to Brigadier General in the Civil War and kept the title within his own command. With his battalion were five companies of roughly fifty troopers each. Another battalion was led by Major Marcus Reno and contained around two hundred cavalry soldiers. The final battalion, which was kept in reserve with the pack train, was led by Captain Frederick Benteen and had three small companies totaling around one hundred men.

Reno began the fight by charging the Sioux encampment, but was quickly repulsed and took refuge in the woods. There he went mad (by most accounts) after one of his scout's brains were blown all over his face. Reno wasted valuable time mounting and remounting his troops insanely before the group finally routed. The survivors rallied with Benteen's reserves on a series of bluffs overlooking the Bighorn and were besieged there through the night.

Custer evidently ran into the main force as they rallied from Reno's attack. Benteen and Reno could hear his battle in the distance, but did not feel able to come to his support. "Yellow Hair's" troopers died to a man. Reinforcements arrived and found the bodies the next day. Most of the soldiers had been horribly mutilated, both by Sioux warriors and by the women and children who came to scavenge their belongings.

Prior to the battle, Sitting Bull experienced a vision of defeating the United States soldiers. That is where history ends and this story begins. In this setting, Sitting Bull's vision did not simply prophesy the defeat of the U.S. Army expedition, it actively told him how to destroy the entire white race! The vision was provided by an evil spirit—a manitou in Sioux terms. It told Sitting Bull that the Great Chief's enemies could be destroyed by an ancient and forbidden ritual. But the ritual required two blood sacrifices. One was a bloody massacre of the invoker's enemies. For the second, Sitting Bull cut off one of his own fingers with Custer's Bowie Knife. Sitting Bull then waited while his people finished the wounded and mutilated their remains.

A short time later, the ritual was complete. Sitting Bull stood, woozy from loss of blood, the excitement of his victory, and the strain of the dark ritual he had cast. He and his people took what they wanted from the fallen soldiers, then moved on to help those Indians who had besieged Benteen and Reno.

That night, as the commander of Custer's column, General Alfred Terry, tried to figure out where he had gone wrong, shouts came in from the pickets. Terry raced out of his tent in time to see a nightmare made real—the troopers of the 7th Cavalry had risen from their graves. The dead things swarmed over the rest of the camp and killed what they could catch before the rest scattered to the four winds.

Those who were wounded by the living dead eventually succumbed to infection and joined the ranks of their fallen comrades. These fiends then turned on those who had taken them in—isolated settlers, border towns and even Forts Fetterman, Laramie, and Benton. Within weeks, Sitting Bull's secret curse became an epidemic, spreading to Cody, Wyoming and Deadwood, South Dakota. The undead now number in the thousands.

It was weeks before Sitting Bull realized exactly what he had done. The manitou had tricked him. The plague had taken the whites as the spirit had promised, but the ravenous undead left in their wake would surely destroy the tribes as well. His own people did not return from the Hunting

Grounds and join the white hordes, but they were attacked and devoured by the vile white zombies just as any other human.

Most of the dead are lumbering simpletons when prey is not about. They scrounge for living flesh in a random fashion, most times settling for trapped livestock or living off any group of survivors they manage to overrun. As the game begins, the dead are learning that a vast source of fresh meat remains untouched in the Sioux "larder." Now hungry patrols of undead cavalry or bands of grisly settlers scour the Dakotas looking for "red meat."

Custer's dead—the first to rise—are clever killers blessed with more intelligence than the other risen dead in this setting. They hunt as a pack, know how to set traps and ambushes, and are masters of mobile war. They hunt their prey with bloodthirsty abandon as their hatred for life is overshadowed only by their hatred of Indians.

Besides their preternatural intelligence, Custer's command was also given another gift by the manitou. The troopers ride undead mounts, hunting red men wherever they can find them.

# The Undead

The zombies in this setting go through the motions of their former lives. Blacksmiths pound on cold iron, trains continue to run (though on no discernible schedule) and cavalry soldiers patrol the plains aimlessly. These actions continue somewhat as normal—until the dead sense potential prey. At that point, the zombies become clever like wolves. They can speak in simple, hate-filled phrases and a rare few can even be somewhat deceptive. The grating voice of their decaying vocal folds almost always gives them away, however.

# The Dance Begins

The setting features the characters as members of the same tribe within the Sioux Nations. Below is some basic information on the Sioux to help the players create their characters and to acquaint the Zombie Master with enough basics of Indian life to run a plausible campaign.

## Dancing Zombies

**Strength** 2    **Intelligence** 1
**Dexterity** 2    **Perception** 1
**Constitution** 2    **Willpower** 1
**Dead Points** 15    **Speed** 4
**Endurance Points** n/a    **Essence Pool** 9

**Attack:** Bite D4 x 2(4) slashing damage or by weapon type

**Weak Spot:** Brain (6)

**Getting Around:** Life-like (3), The Lunge (3)

**Strength:** Dead Joe Average (0)

**Senses:** Like the Dead (0), Scent Tracking (1)

**Sustenance:** Weekly (4), All Flesh Must Be Eaten (0)

**Intelligence:** Tool Use 1 (3)

**Spreading the Love:** Only the Dead (-2)

**Power:** 29

The 7th Cavalry: Custer and his original cavalrymen also have the Teamwork Aspect, adding four points to their Power level. These undead stalk the high plains, riding undead horses (see p. 32) and attempting to rid it of life and particularly their rivals, the Sioux. The hatred of the Indians continues to burn in what remains of the 7th's consciousness. They pursue them relentlessly, torture them, and finally devour their flesh—preferably while their hearts still beat. Custer especially wants to devour Sitting Bull and Crazy Horse, whom he holds personally responsible for his ignoble fate.

**Dances with Zombies**

## The Sioux

The word "Sioux" is used in this campaign because it is the one most players are familiar with. In truth, the word Sioux is derivative of a Chippewa word for "enemy." (Many Indian tribes were "named" by whites asking their foes their names.) In truth, the Sioux had no encompassing name for the people who made up their ranks—primarily the Lakotas, Nakotas, and Dakotas. All spoke the same language and very likely were one tribe at some point in the unrecorded past. By the time the white man ventured across the plains, however, they had broken into three distinct clans divided by the regions they lived in.

At this time, the Lakota are the largest and most influential of the tribes. They are subdivided into seven tribes. In order of size, they are Hunkpapa, Oglala, Burnt Thigh (or Brulè in French), Minneconjous, Sihasapa (Blackfeet), Itazipacola (or Sans Bows in French, which means "no bows"), and Oohenupa (Two Kettles). The Hunkpapa is made up of about thirty families; the Oohenupa contains seven.

The Sioux share a common council of elders called the Wicasa Yatapickas. The most senior leader is Sitting Bull. The Wicasas, and Sitting Bull in particular, enjoy complete authority. Any who challenge them may be exiled or even put to death. Tribal justice is quick and severe. Should the Zombie Master feel it is appropriate, a brave who violates tribal law with good reason may be given a test to prove he was guided by the Great Spirit. Such tasks usually involve single combat with a bear, counting coup on a dead man (touching a zombie with a short club or "coup stick" in hand-to-hand combat), or a physical challenge of some sort.

It is important to remember that the "Sioux Nations" are not formally organized. Every tribe has its own chief (or sometimes chiefs) and some families even consider themselves separate tribes. Even a "tribe" such as the Miniconjou is actually made up of several smaller "tribes," each led by its own chiefs. This has caused whites as much trouble as it has the Indians themselves. No central power means that a treaty signed by one chief has no bearing on the other tribes of the region (though many chiefs claimed they spoke for the Nations). Sitting Bull claimed he never broke a treaty because *he* never signed one (though the "Sioux" did on several occasions).

At this time, the most powerful tribe is the Hunkpapa Sioux. The Hunkpapa have several chiefs, but Sitting Bull is by far the most influential. Generally, the rest of the allied tribes making up the Nations rally to his side when they agree with his decisions, but may openly flaunt his authority when they do not.

There is one exception to this rule. Each summer, the tribes assemble for the Sun Dance. There, four "shirt wearers," or Wicasa Yatapickas, convene their annual assembly. The Wicasas are the four most revered leaders of the Sioux. During the Sun Dance, they have authority over the tribes and are generally able to rule without question. They decide on issues of security, rule on judgments made by lesser chiefs throughout the year, and decide on other major issues concerning the tribe. These rules are considered binding, but a few months and many miles later, the lesser tribes are prone to forget the intent of the elders.

At the lowest level of each "tribe" are 2-30 family groups led by a single chief. His authority is no more binding than the Wicasas, but since he is present with his people year-round, his authority is much more practical. Members who go against the chief's will are dealt with severely. Justice is swift and the accused are often guilty until proven innocent. Punishment among the Nations is particularly harsh. The Sioux enjoy torturing and humiliating their enemies. Their cruel (by white standards, at least) justice extends to members of their own tribe as well.

## Religion

The many people who make up the Sioux have just as many beliefs about how the world of spirits works. The Lakota beliefs are fairly typical however and the information below should provide players with enough background to properly play their characters.

Sioux believe in a great spirit called Wakantanka. The Great Spirit is responsible for all things. He made the earth and sky and all the things in it. Wakantanka made the animals first so that they could prepare the way for his chosen, the people.

Just below Wakantanka are the Four Directions. Each of these represents different forces of nature, and are prayed to for specific boons. East is where the sun comes from, bringing light, wisdom and understanding. The South brings warmth for growing. West is where the sun sets and day ends. It represents the end of life or ways of life (such as the dwindling buffalo herds). North is where the cold winds of winter come from. A warrior about to enter battle might pray to the East for wisdom in battle or to the North to make his heart cold and unforgiving like the December wind.

The annual Sun Dance is one of the Sioux's most important rituals. Certain respected braves dance around a sacred cottonwood tree and give away gifts to the most needy members of the tribe, usually widows, orphans, or those with physical or mental disabilities. The next day, the dancers fast and purify themselves in a sweat lodge. Later (sometimes days later at the discretion of the Wicasas), the braves pierce their skin with eagle claws or sharp sticks tied to the tree by a long, leather cord. The dancers then blow whistles of eagle bone and pull on the cords until the piercing is torn from their chest. They then return to their tribes where their savage wounds are tended by their families. This sacrifice of the flesh is meant to appease the Great Spirit. The dance ends with the leader of the Sun Dance smoking a sacred pipe and praying to Wakantanka. The pipe is then passed about and the dancers retire to the sweat lodge to purify themselves once again. The Sun Dance ends with a massive feast where the dancers are honored and given gifts.

As mentioned above, the Sun Dance also serves as a "governmental convention" of sorts as well. While the dance is going on, the elders of the tribes meet to hear the justice and wisdom of the Wicasas, deal with issues that affect all the people (such as the encroachment of the whites), and record their history. The latter is particularly important as it is the only written record of the Sioux's legacy. Years are named not as dates but for important events, such as "Crushed a Witapahatu's Head," which concerns a failed treaty between the Sioux and the Kiowas over the Black Hills that resulted in violence (1814). Another year was called "The Sun Died" after an eclipse in 1869. At the Sun Dance, the elder Indians recount their most important deeds and the Wicasas decide what

Dances with Zombies

the name of the new year will be. It is interesting to note that in the real world, the Sioux called 1876 "Went to Make a Treaty," rather than lauding their victory over Custer.

## The Four Virtues

The Sioux try to live their lives by four guiding virtues: courage, generosity, reverence, and wisdom. The Sioux words for these values (in order) are *wacantognaka, woohitika, wowacintanka* and *woksape*. Those braves who best portray these values become important war leaders and chiefs. Like any society, however, "politicians," fast-talking masters of manipulation, are equally likely to weasel their way into important positions by interpreting their versions of the four virtues.

## Medicine Men

Shamans of both sexes play large roles in Sioux life. They oversee births, advise on the weather, and bless crops, hunts, and warbands. Medicine men are expected to commune with the nature spirits and help the Sioux in all their spiritual matters. Rules for playing medicine men are given later in this chapter (see p. 108).

## Clothing

The Battle of Little Bighorn happened only a few months prior to the opening of this story, so many of the tribe still wear trophies of the encounter—cavalry hats, jackets, even body parts of the fallen 7th are common. The rest of the Sioux's garb is a mixed affair of buckskins and white clothes given to them by the Indian Agency.

## Food

The Sioux live primarily on buffalo, a herd animal in short supply by 1876. For years, whites have over-hunted the animals, killing entire herds with no thought to managing their numbers. Passengers on trains would even shoot the animals for sport, never even considering using the meat or pelts. The famous Buffalo Bill was so named because he had killed hundreds of the beasts for the meat companies.

The Indians call the buffalo *tatanka*. The animal itself is not sacred, but its "spirit" is revered because nearly every part of the beast is either edible or used as tools or clothing. Hides were used to make everything from teepee covers to moccasins, and bones made hoes, needles and shovels.

The Sioux always grew or cultivated small crops of fruits and vegetables, and are more dependent on their small farms since being placed on reservations. Most of their food prior to the epidemic, however, came from government handouts via the Indian Agency. As one might imagine, most young braves in the tribe are furious at their people's increasing dependence on the white man.

## Gender and Marriage

Women are held on a separate but equal plane. It is their job to gather food (as opposed to hunting), prepare food and clothing, and tend to the young. Men are allowed to marry more than one woman, and are actually expected to marry the widow of a fallen brother so that the woman has someone to support her and her children.

Even homosexuals and transvestites have a place in Sioux society. While not equal to "other" men or women, they were cared for and served as part of the tribe like everyone else. Such individuals are called *winktes*. They wear women's clothes and live their lives as women. Many Sioux-labeled *winktes* may instead have simply been over-protected by mothers afraid of losing their sons in battle. Particularly sensitive or passive individuals may also have been labeled "sissies" by the war-like culture of the Plains Indians. Lesbianism is not part of any historical Sioux records and no word for such women exists. Most likely, women who engaged in such activities kept their business to themselves. The nature of Sioux life, where the man provided the basic necessities for his women, likely prevented lesbian couples more so than any social or official attitude. Lesbian activities, on the other hand, may well have been rampant as the men were often gone for extended periods of time.

## Weapons

Many of the Sioux at Little Bighorn were better armed than the 7th Cavalry. Custer's men carried single-shot Springfield "Trapdoor" carbines, the first standardization since the Civil War. Some Sioux already had repeating rifles, notably the Winchester '73. These were highly prized among the tribes with likely around two hundred available in the entire Sioux Nations—most of those in the hands of the war parties at the Little Bighorn. Repeaters were especially valued not only for their high rate of fire, but the ability to fire from horseback, something few ever managed with muzzle-loaders. It was illegal to sell arms to Indians. Selling them repeaters sent out alarms to the military enforcers right away. Still, it was a big country and many whites made small fortunes selling arms to the Indians to use against their own countrymen.

Many more Sioux had single-shot carbines, bought or taken in battle or raids. Unfortunately for the Indians, they were terrible marksmen, primarily due to lack of training and perhaps the newness of *maza wakan* (firearms or "holy iron") to their culture.

The rest of the tribe, perhaps 40% to 50% at the Bighorn, still carried bows. These were surprisingly effective for several reasons. First, an archer could fire far faster and more accurately than a trooper armed with a single-shot weapon. A large number of victims were hit by three to seven missiles. Second, the lack of powder meant that arrows could be loosed from cover, keeping the archer hidden from his opponent. Finally, arrows could be "lobbed" over small hills and other cover, so that even troopers in cover were vulnerable to massed fire. As was explained in **Chapter Two: The Good, the Bad, and the Dead** (see p. 36), arrows are not particularly lethal unless they hit a major organ, but in a fight, even a mild injury can take a trooper out of action and render him ineffective. Indian arrows by 1876 are primarily made of iron and have barbed tips. Removing one requires three Success Levels on an Intelligence and First Aid Task, or two Success Levels on an Intelligence and Medicine (Surgery) Task. Failure results in D6 additional points of dam-

age per attempt. The doctor can keep digging as long as he wants—he simply risks causing the patient additional injury with each attempt. For roleplaying purposes, removing a barbed arrow generally involves pushing it through the other side—an extremely painful procedure.

Indians generally fared better in hand-to-hand combat with the cavalry than in extended duels with longarms. Tomahawks and clubs were still fairly common, as were large knives, all of which were well-suited to fighting troopers armed mostly with clubs (their carbines could not easily be reloaded once a brawl began). A few braves retained lances as well, though these were falling out of favor during the 1876 campaign as some felt the long reach of the weapon was dishonorable. Still, a warrior armed with a lance could make a brutal opening attack as the charge and power of his horse was likely to drive the weapon clear through an opponent.

## Making Characters

The heroes of this tale should all be members of the Sioux Nations. The particular tribe is unimportant, but the Cast Members should all be of the same group. Most should be braves, but women and medicine men are also important and viable allies.

It is also possible to play white heroes who have befriended the Sioux and somehow proven immune to Sitting Bull's curse, but such characters should be rare. Half-breeds also make interesting characters. As for the zombie curse, characters will not rise from death as long as a portion of his heritage is on the Native American side.

If the Zombie Master allows it, some of the characters might be whites who escaped the undead hordes (scouts, buffalo hunters, and even former lawmen fit this mold). White women might have been "captured" by the tribe when they were young and raised as Indians. Cast Members may also be Indians from other tribes who have been taken in by the Sioux through circumstance (usually violence). The player should do the appropriate research on his chosen tribe, customs, and traditions to help the Zombie Master run his character.

## Restricted Skills

Indian characters may not have any of the skills prohibited in **Chapter Two: The Good, the Bad, and the Dead** of this book (see p. 30). In addition, they should not have Demolitions, Disguise, Driving (Wagon), Engineer (Any), Humanities (Any), Lock Picking (Any), Mechanic, Medicine, Piloting (Any), Sciences (Any), Streetwise, or Writing (Any).

## Recommend and Required Skills

All Native American males must have Survival (Plains) 2 or better, some sort of Hand Weapon 2 or better, Riding (Horse) 1 or better, and Myth and Legend (Sioux) 1 or better. Women may ignore the Hand Weapon skill requirement. These skills are not free; they must be paid for as usual. They are part of growing up in the tribes and so must be purchased during character creation.

## Medicine Men

Cast Members who want to play Medicine Men use the Inspired Character Type presented in the *All Flesh Must Be Eaten* rulebook (see p. 28, 62-66). These shamans draw their energy from nature spirits. Like nature itself, these creatures are cruel and demanding, but powerful and savage in their fury.

To call upon the spirits, shamans offer pledges to protect and honor nature. Thus calling on a Miracle is relatively fast and simple work. Later, when there is more time, medicine men spend much time proving the truth of their pledges. This is when the shaman's various rituals are performed (and in game terms, their power to perform future miracles returned).

There are two important differences in the way Medicine Men work magic.

The first is that the Visions Miracle may only be used after performing a peyote ritual. No Essence is spent, however, as the peyote ritual is more than penance enough. To start, the Medicine Man must gather a half-pound of peyote—a hallucinogenic plant found in the wild. This is a Research/Investigation Task requiring at least two Success Levels. Next, the Medicine Man takes his peyote to an isolated location, such as a mountain peak, mesa, or sacred spot. He may take his chosen weapon, but he may not take food, water, or other necessities. At the location, the Medicine Man prepares a pipe and smokes the peyote. He is expected to continue smoking (if he is conscious and able) throughout the next 24 hours. Each day spent in visionquest, the Medicine Man must succeed in a Ritual Task. Should he fail, he suffers D10(5) damage, times the number of days spent questing.

A single day spent in this way answers simple questions: will a woman have a boy or girl, will a brave live through a particular battle, and so on. More difficult questions require two or more days of fasting and delirium. Sitting Bull once performed a vision quest that took an entire week. His vision foresaw the Battle of Little Bighorn and may well have changed history in the real world. The Zombie Master should use this as a guide to how many days the character must quest before the spirits answer his questions.

Visions are always shrouded in mystery and ambiguity. They are more a riddle than a dream. Suppose a shaman wishes to know a safe spot where his village might hide their women and children from the dead. The vision might involve a talking buffalo that discusses the weather. The Medicine Man eventually rises from his delirium and on his way back to the tribe, hears a buffalo howl in the distance. He finds the herd, then follows them to a sheltered valley far off the beaten path.

The other major change to the Miracles of the Inspired in Dancing with Zombies concerns the recovery of Essence. Normal Essence returns at the rate of the character's Willpower every five minutes (for Inspired characters). Essence spent to cast Miracles, however, may only be recovered by performing rituals. The player must track such Essence losses separately. Below is a list of the most common methods and how much Essence is recovered. The number following the "Essence Recovered" entry is given as a die type to produce a random number. The number in parentheses is the amount recovered if the Zombie Master wants a more predictable result.

### Dance

**Essence Recovered:** D10(5)

**Time Required:** Ten minutes, may only be performed once per day

A quick and simple dance requires little more than simple fetishes and pledges to the nature spirits.

### Formal Dance

**Essence Recovered:** 2D10(10) per participant

**Time Required:** Two hours, may only be performed once per week

Large formal dances require at least one hour of preparation. This time is spent gathering minor fetishes from the wild, starting a fire, and painting certain symbols on the participants' faces and bodies. At least three other braves and/or Medicine Men must participate in the ceremony. The Essence recovered is significant, but more importantly, every Medicine Man involved in the ceremony recovers lost Essence.

### Self-Mutilation

**Essence Recovered:** Special

**Time Required:** One Turn

Sioux Medicine Men often sacrifice their bodies for the greater good of the tribe. The effects of their self-mutilation is to gain extra favor with spirits. Doing so requires the Medicine Man have some way to injure himself. Such wounds should never be life-threatening and cannot be treated with First Aid. Every two Life Points inflicted gives the shaman one Essence Point. The Medicine Man can harm himself as much and as often as he likes. In extreme cases, the Zombie Master might allow a desperate shaman to cause himself greater injuries for more Essence. Should the Inspired offer his life to the spirits, he should be granted Essence on a one-to-one basis for his Life Points—though he expires immediately after completing his last miracle.

### Painting

**Essence Recovered:** Special

**Time Required:** Special

The nature spirits seem to enjoy pictorial representations of themselves and the struggles of man. The more elaborate the picture, the more favor shines down upon the Inspired painter. Most pictures are drawn on teepees, rocks, or static objects. Some shamans prefer to paint on their own bodies and a few have mastered the art of sand painting (spreading colored sand to create intricate patterns). The amount of Essence depends on the difficulty and intricacy of the work.

| Essence Recovered | Painting |
| --- | --- |
| D10(5) | Temporary tattoo, simple painting on a static object |
| 2D10(10) | Detailed painting, small but permanent tattoo, simple sand painting |
| 3D10(15) | Epic painting, large and permanent tattoo, or complex sand painting |

## Starting the Campaign

The story starts in late September of 1876. In the real world, the United States Army had mobilized against the Sioux. In this Deadworld, however, the zombie epidemic has made the white man strangely silent. As winter begins in the cold north, an unholy war is about to begin.

Playing a Sioux Indian is very likely a challenging prospect for most gamers. There is little familiarity with this lost culture and today's attitudes make most see the Indians as either noble savages or persecuted victims interested only in worshiping nature. The information given in this chapter should hopefully remind the players that the Sioux, like any stereotyped group, were people just like any other. Some were noble, others were savage and cruel, all were human. Prior to running the game, it might be a good idea to get the group together and watch a movie such as *Dances with Wolves* that paints a more even and detailed picture than the classic Westerns most readers are familiar with.

Once everyone has made characters, each player should state his name and how he earned it. Obviously, White Killer is going to have a different background than Eats Yellow Snow.

The Cast Members should then be assembled into a warband and sent off to deal with a local threat, such as a group of murderous rogues condemned by the Wicasa Yatapickas. These men, other Sioux, Kiowa, Crow, or Cheyenne, have violated the laws of the Wicasas and are condemned to death. Braves in the party are sent to fight them, while any women are sent to help gather certain items or relics stolen by the exiles. Should the group contain a Medicine Man, he has been sent by an elder shaman who had a vision that an event of great import would happen during the mission. The medicine man is sent to witness and study it.

After the fight, one of the rogue survivors lives long enough to warn his "honored foes" of the coming of white demons with mighty magic who cannot be killed. Most likely, the players believe the brave has not fought whites before and is one of the isolated few who still believe the white man's technology is magic.

The Zombie Master can lull the players even deeper into this subterfuge by letting them come across a group of (living) white hunters rushing across the prairie. The hunters are paranoid refugees who attack the Indians on sight. The Cast Members should win and the players' belief that the rogue was simply a "superstitious savage" is reinforced.

On their way back to the village, the Sioux come upon a small group of soldiers sitting around a campfire. They have no guard that the Sioux can see, but several horses (all undead; see p. 32). The soldiers also have three Indians (two women and an injured brave) tied to a nearby log. Old memories of camp life remain, so the zombies plan on cooking their meat over a spit then devouring it (though not before it is actually dead—the troopers like their meat "extra rare").

The heroes should attempt a rescue and can then realize the truth of the rogue Indians' warning. The troopers are indeed undead blasphemies, though not members of Custer's 7th Cavalry. Assuming they survive, the Cast Members must then try to warn the rest of the Sioux. Their fellows have had much experience fighting the whites, however, especially after the Little Bighorn and laugh at the braves' tales of dead men who will not die.

## Trappers

The first minor quest in the campaign is to prove to the Cast Members' immediate tribal group that the undead do indeed walk among the living. Though there are many ways to do so, the heroes' most likely course is to trap and capture some of the dead things (note that bringing back a decayed corpse is proof of nothing).

## Sitting Bull

Assuming the braves are successful in trapping a dead white man, their chief then asks the heroes to take the proof to the most powerful chief of the Hunkpapa, Sitting Bull. The Wicasa Yatapicka is difficult to meet as he is likely off on a raid or on "important business" elsewhere. The group has to track the elusive chief into the Black Hills where, unknown to anyone else, he is seeking a way to undo his horrible mistake. On the way to Pa Saha, however, the heroes have their first encounter with a large group of undead—miners based in nearby Deadwood. This group is sparsely armed but large and voracious.

Surviving this brief encounter, the party is rewarded by finding Sitting Bull. The Wicasa Yatapicka is in the Black Hills with his personal guards, the Brave Hearts. He fades in and out of coherence thanks to the blood loss and fasting of his vision quest. The Wicasa is of course aware of the problem already, but is impressed by the braves' deeds. The Brave Hearts must stay to protect Sitting Bull in his weakened state, but the chief is looking for a select and trustworthy group for another important task. Sitting Bull realizes the people of the Nations are doomed if they do not band together as they did in the fight against Custer. Gathering the tribes is a significant challenge, however, as the annual Sun Dance already occurred a few months back. Besides the fact that the tribes are nomadic (requiring expert tracking), they must also be convinced to assemble. This is very difficult as the winter has set in and gathering a large group of people when food is scarce is very dangerous.

**Dances with Zombies**

## Too Late

Undaunted, the heroes venture off and stumble upon one family tribe too late. They find the grisly, gnawed remains of men, women and children in their ruined village. Hoofprints from white men's horses are everywhere and bullet holes about the size of those caused by the Springfields are evident. Saber slashes are also common. Most of the bodies have been at least partially devoured. This is an important clue as well as a grisly scene-setter, for the Indians slain by the zombies have not risen as white men killed by the undead do.

Some time after finding the ruined village, the heroes run across Custer and the 7th Cavalry, perhaps spying them from a tall butte. Custer travels with D6 companies of 3D10 troopers each. The Cast Members should not have a major confrontation with Custer at this point—they should just learn that he is out there, hunting the edges of the Sioux Nations for smaller tribes.

## Setting the Table

A few tribes understand the danger of the blasphemous undead and do as Sitting Bull requests. Others are too worried about foraging for food, however, and do not want to risk a trek to an overpopulated campsite in winter. Many are dependent on the Indian Agency's handouts and tell the heroes that the white men have been strangely absent for weeks. To convince these tribes to heed Sitting Bull's command, the heroes must raid a major food source and gather enough resources to feed the members of the chiefs' warbands for at least a month. The Zombie Master can set up any scenario he wishes, but below are the most likely sources of food the Cast Members may target.

**Fort Fetterman, Laramie, and Benton:** These forts have fallen to the undead in the last few weeks, but all were well-stocked with food before the epidemic took hold. Cast Members who make a Simple Intelligence Test know one of the forts' schedule as the Indians often line up to receive their allotments at this time as well. The forts are not as well protected as they were when the troopers inside were alive, and

only around 50 guards remain (the rest were devoured before they could rise). Of course, what the guards lack in discipline, they more than make up for by being dead. Fortunately, the dried meat, vegetables, and other foodstuffs inside have kept naturally cold in the winter and so are still good for another month. Successfully raiding the food stores of any one of these forts supplies a third of the entire gathering for roughly one month (with additional hunting and gathering the tribes will do on their own). Successfully raiding all three forts, then, provides enough food for the entire Nation for one month. Doing so almost certainly makes the Cast Members great and respected heroes to their people.

**Deadwood:** The white settlement at Deadwood is another source of food. Canned goods, dried jerky, and other preserved food can be found in abundance. There is enough stored food here to feed two-thirds of the Nations for an entire month. Unfortunately, there are at least a thousand undead shambling about. Still, a clever party might be able to lure the majority of the zombies away and gather up the scattered supplies given a few wagons and a handful of help.

**Tatanka:** A few buffalo herds remain on the plains as well. Unfortunately, a large camp of buffalo hunters has already gone to the dead side. They hunt slowly but relentlessly, briefly feeding on the raw animal flesh before moving on to slay more of the beasts. Indians who hunt the herd draw the attention of these white men and their large buffalo rifles. There are likely 2D10 of these over-armed undead stalking a herd at any one time. Slaughtering a dozen of these creatures would provide enough meat (and valuable hides) to feed half the Nations for a month.

## Honor of the Hunt

The next phase of the saga begins as growing patrols of dead soldiers and ravenous settlers begin to harass the Sioux. Thanks to the Cast Members' efforts of the past few weeks (or months!), Sitting Bull bestows upon them a great honor. He makes them members of the Brave Hearts' Hunting Society and tasks them with leading the war parties against the pale-faced horrors. The campaign is now in the players' hands.

Gathering the tribes for centralized protection for more than a month is not really an option because of the food situation. There are perhaps 100,000 Indians in the Nations, requiring a huge amount of land for foraging and hunting. This means the heroes must go on the offensive. Should they attempt to ambush the undead in small groups? Or might the heroes try to persuade the Sioux Wicasas to band together and destroy the nearby forts where most of the dead men come from? The Cast Members might also learn that the "iron horses" from Back East cart trainloads of reinforcements and settlers to the West each week. These are quickly killed by the undead and added to the horde. If the Sioux could destroy the trains, they might stem the flow of fresh zombies for a while, perhaps giving them enough time to round up and destroy large groups of them at Deadwood or the forts.

The Zombie Master should allow the players to plot their own attacks. As long as they are successful and avoid treading on the Wicasa's toes, they should get most of the support they need. Other warbands do as they are asked, as do medicine men and even the women and children of the tribes. Regardless, a few difficult individuals find fault with the braves' plan no matter how good it is. The Zombie Master can use these individuals as lesser enemies to add a little variety and diplomacy to the heroes' challenge.

# Complications

Below are a few complications the Zombie Master can use once the campaign against the undead has begun.

## Indian Allies

Once the heroes have united the Sioux, they might think about contacting other Indian tribes. As the Medicine Men tell them, red men do not rise from death. The largest of the southern tribes, Comanche, Kiowa, and Apache, have held out against the encroaching dead and may prove valuable allies. These tribes are not covered here, but a little research should provide the Zombie Master with all the information needed to properly portray them. A major accomplishment in this campaign would be contacting and forming an alliance with each of these tribes. An alliance of all the major tribes, coupled with the power of their Medicine Men, might even be enough to one day reclaim the West—maybe even all of America given a few generations of hard-fighting.

## Sitting Bull Revealed

At some point, the heroes should discover that Sitting Bull is to blame for raising the dead. This could be accomplished through a vision quest, some detective work (perhaps the Brave Hearts know), or being by Sitting Bull's side should he die and decide to reveal his secret.

What to do with the information is a very touchy issue. Sitting Bull's prominence is the primary reason the tribes have united. Should he be revealed, it might mean splintering the Sioux into their various divisions. This would be truly disastrous as divided, the Nations will fall. Too, Sitting Bull attempted to do the Sioux a great favor. Should he be blamed for being tricked by a crafty manitou?

Even if the heroes decide to keep the secret, others may not. One interesting possibility is to let a jealous and powerful Medicine Man learn the secret. He blackmails Sitting Bull into giving him control of the Nations, then sets out on a reckless course that endangers the entire tribe. The heroes must find a way to kill the medicine man without getting caught or revealing Sitting Bull's secret.

A clever party might blackmail Sitting Bull themselves. If confronted, the Great Chief is likely to give the braves most anything they want. If they do a good job in fighting the horrors and preserving the Sioux, Sitting Bull likely leaves them alone. Should he believe they are jeopardizing the tribe's survival, the chief plots secretly to have them assassinated and foiled at every turn.

Some braves or Medicine Men may think they should reveal Sitting Bull's actions. If that is the case, the other Wicasas almost certainly decide to keep his act a secret so as not to splinter the tribes. If the heroes resist, the Wicasas might well send the Brave Hearts after them—"for the good of the Sioux Nations."

**Dances with Zombies**

# Sioux Brave
## Survivor

**Str** 4 **Dex** 4 **Con** 4
**Int** 2 **Per** 3 **Wil** 3
**LPs** 57
**EPs** 38
**Spd** 16
**Essence** 20

## Qualities/Drawbacks

Acute Senses (2)
Cruel (-1)
Fast Reaction
Time (2)
Good
Luck 3 (3)
Hard to
Kill 5 (5)
Honorable (-3)
Nerves of Steel (3)
Reckless (-2)
Resources
(Miserable) (-4)

## Skills

Brawling 4
Climbing 2
Guns (Rifle) 2
Hand Weapon
(Tomahawk) 5
Intimidation 3
Myth and Legend
(Sioux) 3
Notice 4
Occult Knowledge 3
Riding (Horse) 5
Stealth 3
Survival (Plains) 3
Swimming 2
Throwing 3
Tracking 3

## Gear

Captured Springfield
Carbine with 10 Shells,
Tomahawk

## Personality

I was there when Yellow Hair's soldiers attacked Black Kettle at the Washita. I fought, but was wounded by a soldier's bullet. So I lay there, left for dead, as the soldiers shot and stabbed my wife and children. I crawled away before they began to finish off the wounded, and vowed that Yellow Hair and the other blue-soldiers would pay for their crimes.

For years after I killed every paleface I met. Men, women, even their children fell before the vengeance of the Great Spirit. White men hated me; soldiers hunted me. Even some of my own people sought to turn me in for the white man's gold.

Later, I saw Yellow Hair and his soldiers at the Bighorn. I fought beside Crazy Horse and reveled in his madness. The hills ran red with the blue-soldiers' blood. We killed and killed and killed until not one of them remained. I saw Yellow Hair among his dead, for Crazy Horse had forbidden us to kill him until he was the last. We all wanted him to know our fear. To know our hate. What we did to him I will not tell the young braves. That was the end of him.

Now you say Yellow Hair is back. I know you are lying, for I saw him dead. I will ride with you to destroy these soldiers, but I do not believe your tales of their magic. And it is not the same Yellow Hair who leads him. For he is dead.

## Quote

"In the name of the Wakantanka, die paleface!"

# Medicine Man
## Inspired

**Str** 2 **Dex** 2 **Con** 3
**Int** 4 **Per** 4 **Wil** 5
**LPs** 30
**EPs** 35
**Spd** 10
**Essence** 20

## Qualities/Drawbacks

Attractiveness (Self-mutilation Scars) -3 (-3)
Cruel (-1)
Gift (5)
Honorable (-2)
Inspiration (5)
Resources
(Miserable) (-4)

## Skills

Hand Weapon (Spear) 3
Intimidation 2
Myth and Legend
(Sioux) 3
Notice 3
Occult Knowledge 3
Riding (Horse) 2
Ritual 3
Stealth 2
Survival (Plains) 2
Tracking 2

## Miracles

Blessing
The Touch of Healing
Visions

## Gear

Spear, Fetish

## Personality

Do not tell me of the white men, young one. I was born in the year of the Shifting Stars and old when the sun died. I have watched these white devils invade our land for many moons. My father told me of the time When the White Man Came. But the palefaces have changed now. I sense that. They no longer want just our lands. They want our lives.

You say they are dead. Yes, that is true. But they have always been that way. They see not the sway of the trees or the dance of tatanka. They do not hear the North wind telling them which way to hunt, or listen to the water tell them where the fish are.

But what you say does make sense of a vision I was granted. Wakantanka showed me skeletal buffalo grazing in the wide valley where the red grass grows. I walked toward the strange creatures and saw that the grass they devoured bled and screamed as it was chewed. Could the red grass be our people? "Red men" as the whites call us? Perhaps. But what can it mean?

## Quote

"What would you have me do, young one? Wave my hand and cause the palefaces to die? My magic does not work that way."

**Dances with Zombies**

# CHAPTER SEVEN

# OTHER SETTINGS

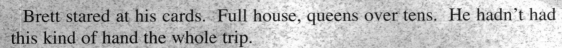

Brett stared at his cards. Full house, queens over tens. He hadn't had this kind of hand the whole trip.

"You got it this time, sugar?" Daisy asked quietly. Brett nodded. She wouldn't give anything away. He had already made the last raise. It was time to reveal his hand.

Two players had already folded. That left General Jeb Cook, a former Confederate officer with one arm (some said his fortune was "foraged" from the war), and Jack "Slim" Morton. It had taken two weeks to get to this point—the last table, the last hand of the biggest poker tournament ever held on the Mississippi. It cost $5000 to get in, and of the fifty contestants, only these five were left. The game took place on the Mississippi Rose, one of the "Bloody Old Muddy's" finer riverboats, and security for the event was so tight it hadn't docked or taken on passengers since the game began.

And that's why it survived the plague.

General Cook flipped over his cards. A flush. He didn't hold out much hope of winning, but on the last hand, he had decided to go for it.

"You're next, son," said Milton Forbes, the owner of the boat and sponsor of the tournament. "Let's see 'em."

Morton smiled and nodded "good luck."

Brett flipped his hand. "Queens and tens, gentlemen."

Cook turned his cards over in disgust and threw down a shot of whiskey.

"What do you have, sir?" said Forbes.

Morton grinned and laid his cards out dramatically, a king, a king, a nine, a nine. . . .

Gunshots sounded outside. A porter suddenly burst into the cabin. "Boarders, sir! They's comin' up in skiffs!"

Shots suddenly rang through the cabin, sending glass flying and men diving to the floor. Something burst through one of the windows—a man—but riddled with bullets and bleeding black blood. Brett saw a feral snarl on the thing's face as it landed on the General and began ripping the flesh of his neck with its bare teeth.

No guns were allowed in the cabin and the hucksters were reluctant to touch the decayed thing. Cook bled like a bucket with a bullet hole in it before someone finally dragged the thing off him. Cook stood quickly and staggered against a window. Another feral face appeared—this one a white woman—and dragged him out into the darkness and his screaming death.

Slim Morton pulled an unseen Derringer form his boot, flashed a half-smile at Brett, then stood. Brett reached out and grabbed his arm. "Wait! I have to know. The last card."

Slim was about to speak when another of the things burst into the room. It landed at Slim's side and tore into his throat like a rabid wolf. Slim kicked up, upsetting the table and launching cards, chips, and whiskey into the air.

"Nooooo!" Brett screamed.

Slim died with a smile on his face. His last bluff.

# Bloody Old Muddy

Bloody Old Muddy starts with the Cast Members on the Mississippi Rose, site of a poker tournament. The characters might be attending the exclusive tournament as players, bodyguards, high-class ladies of the evening, entertainers . . . or even stewards, cooks, and servants. The owner and captain of the boat is Milton Forbes, a millionaire who made his money during the war.

## History

It is now 1870. The war ended five years ago, but the killing has not stopped yet. Unknown to all but a few highly placed former Confederates, the rebels tried several biological weapons before Lee's surrender. One of these was a plague discovered somewhere in the Caribbean. The secret lab where the plague was developed was located near New Orleans at the southern end of the mighty Mississippi. Unfortunately for the Confederate scientists, 19th century technology did not protect them from their own experiments. It wiped them out in their sealed lab and there they lay for over seven years.

A few weeks before the Mississippi Rose debarked, two young boys exploring the myriad swamps of the delta stumbled across the lab and opened its long-sealed doors. The boys, who worked as porters on other riverboats, carried the disease with them up and down the coast for weeks before they finally succumbed to its fatal grip. They were buried, but rose from the grave that very night. Because of the plague's relatively long incubation period (about three weeks), the disease spread quickly among unsuspecting river-folks. Towns and cities along the Mississippi were wiped out in weeks. Now the whole region is rife with the dead and the plague is spreading like wildfire to the east and west. The United States will fall in a matter of months and the entire world may fall within the year.

Fortunately, the first strain of the disease, which spread among the living, did not survive in the land of the dead. The new strain exists only in the undead and can only be transmitted to the living by an exchange of body fluids (such as a bite or occasionally a scratch). This allows the heroes to survive in the aftermath of the plague without worrying about sealed suits (which, of course, are not available in 1870).

Those semi-fortunate souls isolated on the Mississippi Rose are now trapped in a land of the dead. After a few brief attempted landings and several close encounters, Milton Forbes has decided to use his boat as a haven for his guests. His plan is to move up and down the river, landing only when needed to "raid" for food, medicine, fuel and intelligence. They can hold out for at least a year, he believes, by which time he hopes the government will have discovered a solution to this incredible curse.

## The Zombies

The zombies in this setting are usually quite stupid. They go about their previous occupations normally when prey is not about. Undead riverboat captains continue to sail aimlessly up and down river, hunters hunt and soldiers guard posts long since wiped out by the plague. When fresh meat approaches, however, the dead become savage and cunning in their quest for sustenance.

## Milton Forbes

The captain of the Rose is Milton Forbes, one of the rare Southern industrialists. He made a fortune smelting cannons during the war. Forbes' Atlanta home was burned in General Sherman's "March to the Sea," so after the war, he spent a sizeable portion of his remaining funds on the Mississippi Rose. He planned to spend the rest of his life here in relative luxury while playing poker and forgetting about the horrors of the war.

### Bloody Old Muddy Zombie

**Strength** 2     **Intelligence** -2

**Dexterity** 1     **Perception** 1

**Constitution** 2     **Willpower** 2

**Dead Points** 15     **Speed** 2

**Endurance Points** n/a     **Essence Pool** 6

**Attack:** Bite D4 x 2(4) slashing damage

**Weak Spot:** Spine (5)

**Getting Around:** Slow and Steady (0); The Lunge (3)

**Strength:** Dead Joe Average (0)

**Senses:** Like the Dead (0)

**Sustenance:** Occasionally (2); Braiiiiiins (-3)

**Intelligence:** Dumb as Dead Wood (0)

**Spreading the Love:** One Bite and You're Hooked (2)

**Power:** 14

## Milton Forbes

**Strength** 2      **Intelligence** 3
**Dexterity** 2      **Perception** 3
**Constitution** 2      **Willpower** 2
**Life Points** 26      **Speed** 8
**Endurance Points** 23      **Essence Pool** 14

**Qualities:** Attractiveness +1, Resources (Well-off)

**Drawbacks:** Honorable 3, Obsession (Avoid talk about the war)

**Skills:** Bureaucracy 3, Cheating 4, Demolitions 1, Gambling 5, Guns (Handgun) 2, Haggling 3, Intimidation 3, Language (French) 3, Notice 2, Piloting (Riverboat) 3, Smooth Talking 3, Swimming 3

**Gear:** Derringer, Pack of Playing Cards

## Scenes

Here are a few key scenes for this setting. The Zombie Master should allow the players to decide their own basic strategy and work these ideas into the game as time goes on.

**Beans and Bullets:** The first thing the group needs is more guns, ammunition, and food. Forbes is happy to release the personal weapons collected from the players, but most of those who were "heeled" carried only pistols. The crew is armed with rifles (for protecting the loot), but they used up most of their 20 bullets a piece on the first wave of zombies that tried to board.

Forbes (or one of the Cast Members) proposes a raid on a local Union garrison still in place to keep the peace after the war. Of course, the troops posted there are now walking dead, and well-armed walking dead at that. The fort might even have its cannons operable. These devastating weapons were designed to destroy warships running the Mississippi gauntlet, so they can tear the Rose to splinters in a few shots. The group must come up with a clever plan to land the boat nearby and attack the fort from the land.

For food, the crew and characters can go hunting along the banks of the Mississippi. Animals do not catch the strange disease (even when wounded), but while off the boat, the heroes are likely to find themselves hunted by the many bands of roving zombies stalking the shores. These cat and mouse games take the heroes through dark cypress swamps, to ruined plantations or along sandy river ways.

**The Duel:** The Rose is cruising along when it comes across a riverboat foundered on a shallow sandbar. Circling the vessel are scores of undead. A few desperate humans fight them off, firing from the slanted decks of the boat. The group avoided the initial stages of the plague just like the passengers of the Rose. Unfortunately, their pilot and captain have died in their struggle, and none of the remaining passengers and crew know how to pilot the boat. They tried anyway but quickly foundered on a sandbar. The group was discovered by the dead three days ago and no matter how many they kill, dozens more show up soon after—no doubt attracted by the gunshots and the smell of blood in the air and in the water.

## Desdemona Sharpe

**Strength** 2     **Intelligence** 2
**Dexterity** 2     **Perception** 4
**Constitution** 2     **Willpower** 4
**Life Points** 26     **Speed** 8
**Endurance Points** 29     **Essence Pool** 16

**Qualities:** Attractiveness +3, Photographic Memory

**Drawbacks:** Honorable -3, Minority (Woman), Recurring Nightmares

**Skills:** Beautician 3, First Aid 3, Gambling 3, Guns (Handgun) 3, Guns (Shotguns) 2, Intimidation 3, Language (French) 1, Notice 4, Play Instrument (Piano) 1, Questioning 2, Riding (Horse) 2, Seduction 3, Smooth Talking 3, Swimming 2

**Gear:** Shotgun with 24 Shells, Dress

Forbes, ever the gallant Southerner, decides to attempt a rescue. Exactly how this happens is up to the group—Forbes is open to suggestions. This might be a great place to bring on love interests, old enemies or even new characters to replace those lost in previous misadventures.

**Fresh Blood:** The heroes are out hunting when they discover a small group of thirteen survivors. These desperate souls proved strangely immune to the virus (or simply entered the area after the first stage of the disease had passed). The survivors are led by a beautiful widow, Desdemona Sharpe.

The dead are everywhere and there are rumors that the virus has gone airborne again. Whether this is true or not is up to the Zombie Master, but it forces the heroes to stay on the Rose. The survivors are low on food, lost and in serious trouble if the Cast Members do not take them in. Of course, that means more mouths to feed. The most ruthless characters may want to abandon them. More heroic types will want to take them in. Either side may become entranced by Desdemona, causing even more tension when deciding the survivors' fate.

Desdemona has recently come from the East and warns the heroes that heading there will only result in their death. She lost her first family in the war, remarried and lost another husband to the plague. The fact that she is still sane and alive is a grim testament to the rock-hard survivor buried beneath her Southern corset. The Tennessee native is blond and trim. She is barely 30 years old, but other than the grim look in her eye, could pass for 25. She is stern and unforgiving when required, and compassionate when possible. Desdemona is sometimes ignored by men when it comes to discussing "important issues" because of her gender and good looks. That rarely lasts, however, as she is quick to show them the error of their ways through knowledge and deeds.

**Impending Doom:** Milton Forbes has a father-complex. He feels it is his duty to protect everyone on board. Forbes refuses to put down or exile a wounded character even once the party knows how the zombies "spread the love." The best Milton will agree to is locking the wounded in a room below.

This development should cause all sorts of complications. The wounded person is not happy about being left untended with a grievous wound of some sort. He (or she if you really want to be cruel to a party likely made up of mostly gallant Southerners) bangs on the door and the ceiling and yells for help and comfort constantly. Maybe some of the other passengers even sneak the victim food, water, or other aid. Eventually, of course, the victim dies and returns as a groaning undead. This actually makes her easier to deal with, but now some of the passengers (if not the Cast Members) want her thrown overboard. Forbes refuses until convinced there is no cure. What happens next depends on the party. Do they keep putting wounded companions in the "zombie room?" How? Do they throw them out at first bite or only after they've died? The moral dilemma of this situation should present some great roleplaying challenges in between bits of action-oriented zombie blasting.

**The Cure:** During one of their foraging trips along the Mississippi, the heroes come across the old Confederate bunker where the disease originated. There they find the scientist's notes and diaries. Within them is the secret to destroying the disease, even in the "dormant" state that keeps the dead walking. To do this requires several key chemicals scattered up and down the Mississippi in various locations. Some are naturally occurring compounds found in certain crops, others are man-made chemicals that might be found in most large cities, such as New Orleans. Of course, these locations are crawling with hordes of hungry undead.

Assuming someone in the group can decipher the notes and the "antivirus" is created, the party must then find a way to distribute it. This can be best done by turning the chemical into a gas. With a little more scrounging, the Mississippi Rose can be fitted with a howitzer to fire chemical shells into river-towns. The heroes could then establish a "beachhead" and begin a systematic extermination of the dead. As they do so, more and more survivors should emerge to help.

"They're all dead, sir."

Lieutenant John G. Broadstone stared at the smoking settlement on the horizon. A half-dozen farms had now fallen to the Comanche raiders. The young man had seen savagery before, but never anything like this. The Comanche were eating their victims.

"More evidence of cannibalism?"

The black sergeant nodded. Sergeant Ethan Evers was a veteran. He'd been fighting the Indians for years now and it was obvious he had never seen anything like this either.

"What are your orders, sir?" Evers asked.

Broadstone shifted in his saddle and checked the horizon. Far to the south was a small dust cloud signaling riders. If the troop rode hard, they might be able to catch them. Of course, it was probably just more settlers, but at least he could warn them to stay together. "Let's make for that dust cloud, Sergeant."

An hour of hard riding later found the troop in the upper stretch of a long draw. A half-mile away, at the bottom of the draw and bordered on either side by steep ridges, was a jumbled collection of covered wagons. Several of the prairie schooners lay on their sides.

"Sergeant, take two men and scout that out. Look for survivors. We're too late."

Evers slapped his Colt and raced off at once, followed by two other veterans of his troop. Broadstone watched through his spyglass as the men approached the wreckage. They started slowly, probing the exterior of what might have been a belated attempt at circling around the two that wrecked. Suddenly, one of the men went down, as if pulled from his horse, but Broadstone could see no Indians. Evers and the other solider fired, but again, Broadstone could see no target. A cloud of dust erupted, and after several agonizing seconds, Evers came busting through, racing back to the troop Hell bent for leather.

Broadstone motioned for the troop to form a line. "Hold your fire until I give the order!" he screamed, expecting to see a mob of Comanche in pursuit of Sergeant Evers. The veteran reined up in less than a minute, his dark black face almost as pale as Broadstone's tan. "What happened, sergeant?" Broadstone yelled in confusion.

"I-I don't know, sir! Comanche, but . . . Private Washington . . . we shot him . . . "

"You shot Private Washington?" Broadstone asked quietly.

"No!" Evers replied. "Shot the Comanche. Three times! He wouldn't die!"

"Behind us, sir!" came a voice from the troop. Broadstone turned and saw a long line of Comanche warriors at the top of the draw. There was something odd about the way they sat on their horses though. They seemed to lurch and jerk on their blankets and the horses seemed oddly still. They weren't stomping and snorting as they usually did on smelling death in the air.

"To the wagons!" Broadstone yelled. "We'll kill whatever's left there and fight from behind the circle!"

Sergeant Evers screamed "No!" but it was too late. The troop was already in motion. He shouted one last time at his lieutenant. Broadstone slowed and urged him on, but Evers still would not follow. He had never disobeyed an order before. "Come on, Ethan!" Broadstone screamed, seeing the Comanche at the top of the draw begin to charge.

Evers shook his head. Then he put his reins in his teeth, drew two pistols, and charged up the chute towards the approaching mob. Lieutenant Broadstone watched just long enough to see the Comanche pull the veteran off his horse and pounce on him—as if they were tearing him limb from limb with their hands and teeth.

## Here Comes the Cavalry

In this Deadworld, the Cast Members are all "buffalo soldiers" in the 3rd United States Colored Regiment of Cavalry. Their usual assignment is to string telegraph poles, patrol the borders of the Indian lands, and bring in any wanted Indians known to be in the area. What the buffalo soldiers don't know is that they're about to become buffalo burgers.

## History

The zombie outbreak began when a man named Moses Mobley found a seam of silver in the Oklahoma outlands. The only problem was that the silver sat just inside an Indian reservation—more importantly, on an ancient Comanche burial ground.

Moses knew the Indians would kill him if they caught him on their burial ground, so he concocted a murderous plan. He gathered blankets from a settlement rife with smallpox, then sold them for a profit to the village. The insidious scheme worked even better than Moses had hoped—the village spread the plague to the entire tribe, wiping out nearly two hundred Comanche in less than two months.

Then the tribe approached the burial ground, bearing their legions of dead. Moses quickly struck camp and hid in the nearby hills, watching as the Comanche buried over a hundred of their fallen kin on his "claim." Moses was shocked as he watched the Indians' "primitive" mourning ceremonies. Scores of horses were slain and left to rot with their former riders. To Moses, the death of so many valuable horses was an appalling loss—the loss of the Comanche lives meant nothing to him.

The Indians finished their ceremonies an agonizing two days later and finally departed. Moses packed up his tools and went right back to work amid the drying husks of dead Comanches and rotting horses.

That night, the dead had their revenge.

The fallen Indians quietly climbed from their burial scaffolds and devoured Moses in a shower of hot blood. The warriors then mounted their horses, covered themselves in bloody "warpaint" and went off in search of revenge.

## The Cavalry

The Cast Members are black cavalry soldiers. Most should be privates or corporals, though one could be the veteran sergeant of the group. One of the heroes could even be the white officer of the troop (a First Lieutenant). This can prove especially interesting, as the players have to get used to taking orders from one of their own play group. The lieutenant has a challenge as well, ordering his friends (through their characters in the game) into mortal danger. Will he bravely lead from the front, risking the troop's leadership and command? Or will he send others into harm's way, ruining his reputation with the men but protecting the integrity of the unit?

Playing the unit's officer can be an incredibly interesting challenge for an experienced roleplayer. Even more interesting is to put the least experienced roleplayer in command and make the veteran players serve as his troopers. This is, unfortunately, very realistic and should highlight some of the difficulties met by courageous veterans led by green officers.

## The Undead

The dead Comanche ride their own horses (see p. 32), slain in the traditional ceremony befitting honored dead. Most were also buried with their personal hand weapons and bows. They had no arrows, but made their own from their burial stands and their own bones. The latter weapons have now become magically cursed like the fiends that use them.

The undead Comanche are not particularly intelligent in most ways, but they have returned with the cunning of wolves. They can set traps, herd their prey into ambushes, and do not rush headlong into prepared defenses.

Because of the magic of the sacred burial ground, the dead Indians cannot venture further than seven miles from the site. The moment a zombie passes this limit, it loses animation and "dies." It is not reanimated if returned to the area or even if interred in the burial ground.

## Scenes

If the heroes are allowed to simply call on the regiment for aid, the undead will not be long for this world. For that reason, the Zombie Master needs to somehow isolate the Cast Members. No calling on the cavalry—they are the cavalry!

This can be done in several ways. The first is to simply have the troops' superiors disbelieve them. Bigoted officers are often looking for reasons to disband the colored regiments anyway, and having the men recite stories of cannibalistic Indians returned from the grave will not help the buffalo soldiers. If a zombie is captured and brought before the regimental commander, the Zombie Master should feel free to have it "play dead." It very likely is if taken more than seven miles from its burial ground anyway. If not, the zombie just allows itself to be destroyed for the "greater good" of its companions.

Another way to isolate the team is to have them surrounded or trapped by the Comanche. Much like Custer's Last Stand, perhaps the troop fights its way into an abandoned (or occupied) circle of wagons, a ranch, a train, or some other protection. The adventure then becomes about escape and survival. This works particularly well as a one-shot adventure. If that is the case, the regiment could respond if some survivors return to tell the tale. Then the story ends and the heroes ride off into the sunset.

In either case, this game should likely only last a few sessions. Making a campaign of this setting is possible, but the dead cannot spread the love and so will eventually be overwhelmed by even a few troops of cavalry. Should the Zombie Master wish to prolong the setting, a particularly powerful Indian shaman hears of the "miracle" and sees the undead as spiritual hunters of his people. The shaman then tries to perform some complicated ritual to allow the dead to spread the love. The medicine man might even be mad enough to get his own people killed to provide more undead troops for his "holy" campaign against the whites. Stopping the shaman might be a mini-campaign in itself, as is cleaning up the after-effects should he be successful.

## Comanche Zombies

**Strength** 4    **Intelligence** -2

**Dexterity** 2    **Perception** 1

**Constitution** 2    **Willpower** 1

**Dead Points** 15    **Speed** 4

**Endurance Points** n/a    **Essence Pool** 10

**Attack:** By weapon

**Skills:** Hand Weapon (Axe, Bow, Club, Knife, Spear, Tomahawk) 2, Riding (Horse) 3

**Weak Spot:** Heart (6)

**Getting Around:** Life-like (3)

**Strength:** Strong Like Bull (5); Damage Resistant (5)

**Senses:** Like the Dead (0); Life Sense (2)

**Sustenance:** Weekly (4); Sweet Breads (Heart) (-3)

**Intelligence:** Tool Use 1 (3); Teamwork (4)

**Spreading the Love:** None (-5)

**Special Abilities:** Bone Arrow (5)

**Power:** 41

### Bone Arrows

The Comanche bone arrows are magically cursed. When the arrow lodges in the flesh of a living person (scores a hit), the bone tip breaks off and begins to rend its way through the body to the heart. This causes D4(2) damage every Turn, and results in death in 2D6 Turns. The only way to stop the heart-seeking missile is to cut it out of the victim within the first three rounds of the injury. This requires Four Success Levels on an Intelligence and First Aid or Medicine (Surgery) Task. Because the surgery must be performed so quickly and brutally, the victim takes D6 damage per attempt regardless of its success or failure. If the Task cannot be performed within three Turns of the injury, the arrowhead has gone too deep into the body and the victim is doomed. The Zombie Master should allow him to go out in a blaze of glory, however.

As this is a very powerful and frankly, unfair, artifact, the Zombie Master should take care to let the Cast Members witness its deadly effect on a Supporting Cast or Adversary first.

The zombies have ten bone arrows each. They can replenish their supply once each night by carving slivers from the bones of their victims. Only the living killed by the Comanche can be used for this purpose.

Canadian Mountie Sergeant-Major Roger Clement stared at the impossible line of Yankees stretched out below him on the portion of the Chilkoot Pass called the "Scales." Since gold had been discovered in the Yukon in '96, the Americans had come to the area by the thousands. The pathetic southerners were used to the relatively mild winters of the American northwest or the almost perpetual warmth of California. They were completely ignorant of the screaming, murderous winds of the North.

"You there," Clement said to a scruffy-looking miner with nothing but a small sack and some ragged furs. "Where are your supplies?"

"Right 'chere," said the man through a mouth full of tobacco.

"The Canadian government is not granting passage to anyone not carrying one year's worth of supplies. You've got barely a week's worth if that in that bag. You'll have to go back."

"I don't need no supplies. I got my rifle in here and I am an excellent shot. I reckon there's plenty o' game to keep a man fed."

"Sorry. Go on back, now. There's a thousand more waiting to get past you."

The man shook his head and proceeded ahead.

Clement put out his arm and touched the man's furs. No doubt they would have been flea-ridden were it not so cold here in the Yukon. "I said turn about. Or we'll escort you out." Two other Mounties checking supplies took notice and watched for trouble.

Sure enough, the man pulled a Derringer from beneath his heavy furs. "Back off, Canuck. I ain't got no reason to kill you, yet, if'n you'll just get out of my way."

Clement sighed. "You're one of Soapy's bunch aren't you?" Soapy Smith was a former Denver-gangster who had over 300 armed men in the American "sheep town" at the start of the Chilkoot trail. Clement had asked for permission to go in and run them out on several occasions, but the Canadian government wanted no trouble with the Americans.

"What if I am?"

"Either he's kicked you out of the gang, you're running from him, or you're after someone who crossed them and made it up the Pass. I'd guess you're the running kind."

The man snarled and cocked his Derringer. "Shut up, Mountie. Or that coat a yours is gonna get a lot redder."

Clement stretched the fingers in his right-hand glove, saw that Soapy looked at it, then struck him across the chin with a sharp left. The Derringer flew into the air and Clement caught it with ease. "We Mounties always get our man, you know."

*\*\**

Sergeant Clement woke up the next morning to a tremendous crash, as if a boat full of dynamite had exploded on the riverbank far below. He rushed into his uniform, pulled up his boots, and threw on his heavy furs as he ran out the door of his post. The lip of the pass was covered with men thrown to the ground. Here and there were spots of red—Mounties on duty through the night. Strange green smoke came from the river valley below the pass, just out of Clement's sight. He moved cautiously to the edge, stopping only to help a dazed trooper stand, and looked in disbelief at the carnage below.

Thousands of Americans and their scattered supplies lay sprawled upon the snowy valley floor. Above them, on a high peak, a portion of the mountain seemed to have exploded.

"It fell from the sky," said the Mountie beside Clement.

"A meteor?" To Clement's surprise, many of the men in the valley below began to rise. The blast from the meteor must surely have killed most, but many seemed to have survived. It was difficult to tell with the heavy green gas seeping from the crater into the valley floor.

"Take a few men and close the pass down below. Check for wounded and set up a hospital. On the American side. The men on the Scales won't last while we tend the wounded, so I'll stay here and pass those from the mid-point up. The rest will have to go down and aid their countrymen. Hurry on now Sergeant."

"Yes, Sergeant-Major," the Mountie said. Clement watched for a few more minutes as the men on the Scales began to rise to their feet. They were heavily burdened with their required year's worth of supplies and exposed to the howling winds. He could not let them sit there long or there would almost certainly be casualties or at least severe frostbite. He passed the first few men quickly, not bothering to check their supplies as thoroughly as he was supposed to, but his practiced eye could tell they carried enough goods for at least ten months.

A few minutes later, Clement heard screams from the base of the valley. He passed by two woefully-unprepared Yanks and stared down into the pass. The "wounded" miners were on their feet and attacking those who stood in line. Clement saw several of his red-coated allies disappear into the swarming mass.

"No one move a muscle," he barked to the miners beside him, knowing full well they'd make for the hills as soon as he was gone. Regardless, the Mountie drew his service pistol and headed down the track toward the commotion. He met Sergeant Moore halfway down.

"S-Sergeant-Major . . ." Moore collapsed, shivering, at Clement's feet as panicked miners tried their best to push past him on the narrow trail. "D-Dead . . . dead men . . . so cold . . ."

Clement sat Moore down gently and cocked his pistol. A few steps further down the steep path brought him face-to-face with a frozen nightmare. A bluish corpse staggered toward him, fresh blood dripping from its mouth and steam rising from its mouth, nose, and eyes. It was the man who had drawn a pistol on him yesterday—one of Soapy Smith's gang. Clement, ever the lawful type, issued a challenge first. "Stop! Stop or I'll shoot!" The Mountie watched as the thing grabbed a passing miner and dug its claws into the back of his neck. The miner screamed, then shivered and groaned as steam rose from his collar. The horror reveled in its feast. Clement fired into its gut. Steam rose in great gouts, melting the snow on the creature's dirty pelt. He fired again and again, but the thing did not stop. The miner in its hands eventually fell to the ground, a shivering mass of flesh surrounded by a stampede of panicked Americans. Clement had one shot left. He fired and hit the thing smack between the eyes. Its head shattered like a hot melon, showering the mass behind with brains and skull. Steam rose from it in great gouts, far too hot for anything human—or once human.

Still, Clement had killed the thing. "We always get our man," he said.

The Sergeant-Major's blood froze as he saw a thousand more of the horrors ascending the Scales.

# North, to Alaska

North, to Alaska takes place on the last great frontier of the West—the Yukon area of Canada and Alaska. The heartlands of the United States are vast and many areas are inhospital. Many stories of the West center around the challenges posed by the frontier environment. But these Great Plains, Rocky Mountain or even Death Valley locales are veritable picnic spots compared to the endless and man-killing terrain of the Great White North.

The frigid weather and dangerous landscape cannot dissuade the desparate miners streaming North though. Gold has been found in the Klondike and hundreds of thousands of miners have rushed to the region to get in on the action. Unfortunately, a meteor strike has spawned an outbreak of the dead, creating a new type of zombie particularly well adapted to the frigid North. As if the environment were not deadly enough.

## The Alaskan Gold Rush

Gold was found in the Yukon in August 1896 by Skookum Jim Mason, Dawson Charlie and George Washington Carmack. Specifically, the men struck gold along a tributary of the Klondike River in Canada's Yukon Territory.

By 1897, an army of gold diggers flocked to the Yukon in response to newspaper stories that irresponsibly reported gold was lying in the streams for anyone to grab. Most travelers came by way of Seattle, Washington, where they were told the Canadian Government had imposed certain rules on the "stampeders." Most importantly, every gold digger was expected to have one year's worth of supplies. This immense burden was intended to avoid widespread famine and death from the elements among the newly arrived prespectors. No doubt it was also hoped that it would keep many from attempting the long trek North. Canadian Royal Mounties stood watch at all the passes to ensure the law was obeyed.

## Yukon Supplies

The following year's supplies for one man were recommended by the Northern Pacific railroad company in the *Chicago Record's Book for Gold Seekers*, 1897.

150 lbs. bacon

400 lbs. flour

25 lbs. rolled oats

125 lbs. beans

10 lbs. tea

10 lbs. coffee

25 lbs. sugar

25 lbs. dried onions

15 lbs. salt

1 lb. pepper

75 lbs. dried fruits

8 lbs. baking powder

2 lbs. baking soda

1/2 lb. evaporated vinegar

12 oz. compressed soup

1 can mustard

Gold pan

Set granite buckets

Large bucket

Knife, fork, spoon, cup, and plate

Frying pan

Coffee and teapot

Scythe stone

Two picks and one shovel

One whipsaw

Pack strap

200 feet of 3/8-inch rope

Canvas for wrapping

Two oil blankets

5 yards of mosquito netting

3 suits of heavy underwear

1 heavy machinaw coat

2 pairs heavy machinaw trousers

1 heavy rubber-lined coat

1 dozen heavy wool socks

1/2 dozen heavy wool mittens

2 heavy overshirts

2 pairs heavy snagproof rubber boots

2 pairs shoes

4 pairs blankets

4 towels

2 pairs overalls

1 suit oil clothing

Several changes of summer clothing

Small assortment of medicines

1 tin matches (per four men)

Stove (per four men)

Two axes and one extra handle (per four men)

Six eight-inch files and two taper files (per four men)

Draw knife, brace and bits, jack plane and hammer (per four men)

8 lbs. of pitch and 5 lbs. of oakum (per four men)

Nails, five lbs. each of 6, 8, 10 and 12 penny (per four men)

Tent, 10 x 12 feet (per four men)

Other Settings

Steamers carried the hopeful miners to the Yukon where they had to choose from one of several entry points into Canada. The most famous of these was the Chilkoot Trail, an unforgiving climb up steep, snow-covered mountainsides. The trail was near impossible for animals, meaning humans had to bear the incredible load of one year's supplies. And as they had heard in Seattle, the Mounties were there to enforce the law.

Another way into the Yukon was through White Pass. It soon became known as Dead Horse Pass as anxious prospectors overloaded their pack animals and forced them forward through the rough terrain and freezing cold until they died. Many of their corpses litter the bottom of what has come to be called Dead Horse Gulch.

Anyone who did not meet the Mounted Police's requirements was turned away. Many of these settled into the new "landing towns" of Skagway, Sheep Town, or Dyea. These rough, unplanned frontier towns were home to notorious gunmen and thieves. Sheep Town in particular was known as a hotbed of violence. It was under the control of Soapy Smith, a former Denver gangster who controlled a gang of three hundred murderers, rapists, and thieves.

Those who passed the Mounties successfully were often still unprepared for the rough terrain that awaited them. Raging white-water rivers, blizzards, avalanches, and steep mountainsides all stood between the miners and their expected fortunes. The Zombie Master is encouraged to use all of these natural elements against the heroes as they are chased across the frozen plains by the dead.

## The Cast Members

Most of the heroes should be miners, but many famous gunmen and outlaws joined in the Yukon gold rush as well. Sometimes they were just as eager as everyone else to get rich. Other times notorious men simply went north to escape their reputations or wait until the law back home cooled its heels over their latest crime.

Characters who do not want to soil their hands with the back-breaking work of mining might simply be porters or even hired guns. There are known to be large outlaw gangs and claim-jumpers in the region, so able-bodied guards are sometimes hired by wealthier outfits. Such individuals are usually promised a share of any gold struck as well.

Native Inuits might join the party after it has ventured into the wastes. Such folks make great replacements once the group's numbers begin to diminish.

No special Qualities or Drawbacks are required or recommended for this setting. Just about any character type works. The only important thing to remember is that only relatively tough individuals would ever set off into the Alaskan and Canadian wilderness. Women are a rarity and children under the age of 16 or so are never brought along on such a harsh expedition.

Skills are another story. Some of the more important skills for characters are Survival (Arctic), Pilot (Boat), Climbing, Craft (Prospecting), and Tracking (for finding game).

## Cold Zombies

The zombies created by the strange meteor are imbued with some of the characteristics of the cold land that surrounds them. The dead quickly take on a bluish tinge and though dead, steam still rises from their mouths and nose. The things crave heat and can detect warmth with their infravision power up to about thirty feet. Their touch is as icy as their graves should be. Each hit with their frozen claws drains a victim's body heat until the victim is a freezing lump of cracking flesh.

The dead do not seem to have an agenda of any sort. They simply wander the Yukon looking for warm meat to devour. Animals cannot return to life after being drained, but they do provide sustenance when they can be caught.

## Cold Zombies

**Strength** 2      **Intelligence** -2

**Dexterity** 1      **Perception** 1

**Constitution** 2      **Willpower** 1

**Dead Points** 15      **Speed** 2

**Endurance Points** n/a      **Essence Pool** 5

**Attack:** Cold Touch (4)

**Weak Spot:** Brain (6)

**Getting Around:** Slow and Steady (0); the Lunge (3)

**Strength:** Dead Joe Average (0)

**Senses:** Like the Dead (0); Infravision (2)

**Sustenance:** Weekly (4); Special (body heat) (0)

**Intelligence:** Dumb as Dead Wood (0)

**Spreading the Love:** Only the Dead (-2)

**Power:** 22

### Cold Touch

Cold Zombies literally drain the heat from their victims with but a touch, causing D10 Endurance Points. Once a victim reaches zero Endurance Points, she dies. The victim rises within minutes aching for warmth.

# The Action Begins

The heroes should be in line at one of the passes when the dead arise. Chilkoot is probably the most interesting as the only climbable path up the hill is a single-file trail. When the meteor hits and the dead arise (as in the opening fiction), the Cast Members must decide whether to go up or down, and how to fight their way through the swarm. It is important to herd the heroes up the trail and into the wastelands beyond, so the zombies fill the pass and block the exit. A few dozen miners streaming into the dead's bloody, freezing grip should alert the heroes to the futility of running back down the trail.

There are roughly a thousand dead at the bottom of the Scales five minutes after the meteor strikes—the walking corpses of the miners waiting their turn at the trail. It takes a full five minutes for those halfway up the Scales to realize what is happening below. The seven Royal Canadian Mounted Police at the top of the pass try to stage a defense and might even hold out for a while in their log cabin Warden Station. The characters and a few dozen other survivors might join them. Eventually the zombies find a way to crack the strongpoint, however, and the heroes are forced into the wilderness, likely attempting to head for another of the Yukon's many new towns. Unfortunately, the meteor that struck the Chilkoot was but the first of many that now pepper the region. The characters may see the "shooting stars" later that night after a narrow escape from their heat-sensing pursuers at the Scales. If they do not catch on, they are taught to pay more attention to such portents when they approach a settlement that turns out to be inhabited by the dead. Sheep Town, Dyea, Skagway, and all the other areas the heroes are likely to travel to are all struck by the strange meteors and transformed into frigid charnel houses.

Once the characters realize they cannot go east, they might decide to head west across the Yukon and into the settled areas beyond. It is a long trek, but they are well supplied and should be able to make it with a little luck.

## Into the Wilderness

Between the Scales and Skagway (or any other town), the going is fairly easy. There are rough areas, but nothing the heroes can not handle. Once they are forced west, however, the going gets incredibly rough. Worse, they are pursued by ravenous dead and must overcome these harsh obstacles to escape. Below are brief overviews on some of the Yukon's challenges and how to deal with them.

**White Death:** The party hears a sharp crack somewhere above them while trudging up a steep hill. Moments later, several massive boulders of snow come rolling toward them. Within moments, a full-scale avalanche begins. A Perception Task with three Success Levels allows a character to spot a rock outcropping or other possible spot to hide in. The heroes have two Turns to make it into cover before the avalanche descends upon them. This requires Running Tasks at a -2 penalty to account for their bulky clothes. Those who do not make it are swept away and must make a Difficult Strength Test. Failure means the hero is crushed to death and buried in the massive drift. With success, the hero is trapped in the snow and suffocates in roughly half an hour. She may make one Difficult Strength Test to dig herself out, but she only gets one chance.

In any case, the Cast Members' supplies are almost certainly gone. They will have to forage for food or raid a settlement somewhere along the way.

**Raging River:** At some point in their escape, the heroes come to an abandoned cabin along a raging river. A sturdy raft and several paddles are evident (and perhaps a few scant supplies if the party is in need). The zombies descend and the heroes are forced into the water.

Navigating the river requires various Dexerity and Piloting (Raft) rolls. A quick search on the Internet can provide the Zombie Master with some maps of real white-water rivers to add additional detail and realism to the trip.

The zombies, completely immune to the cold, are more than happy to jump into the water and give chase. Navigating the white water is bad enough, but when the dead begin grabbing paddles, pulling men overboard and blocking rapids, the white water may well turn red!

## Bear (Grizzly)

**Strength** 8-10      **Intelligence** 0-1 Animal

**Dexterity** 3-4      **Perception** 2-4

**Constitution** 3-5      **Willpower** 4-6

**Life Points:** ((Strength + Constitution) x 5) + 15

**Endurance Points:** ((Strength + Constitution + Willpower) x 3) + 10

**Speed:** ((Dexterity + Constitution) x 2) + 5

**Essence Pool:** 20-30

**Attack:** Claws D6(3) x Strength slashing damage; Bite D4(2) x Strength + 1 slashing damage

**Skills:** Brawling 3, Notice 3, Tracking 3

**Grizzly!:** The heroes find a cave for shelter, but it turns out to be inhabited by a full-grown Kodiak grizzly. The massive bear charges and attacks. On the plus side, if it can be killed, its pelt should make a warm coat and its meat a filling meal.

**Blizzard:** The Yukon is frequently struck by raging blizzards. Besides the freezing cold, limited visibility means characters may become lost or wander into dangerous terrain, such as cliffs or frozen ponds. Blizzards start fast and hit hard. Characters who make an Intelligence and Survival (Arctic) Task rolls should get about a half-hour's notice. Another similar Task can be made to find adequate shelter. Each search requires a half-hour of time, so one roll may be made before the blizzard hits if the party is alerted. If not, they will have to find shelter after the blizzard hits—a much more difficult prospect (apply a -4 penalty to the Task roll).

Every ten minutes spent in the blizzard costs a properly equipped character one Endurance Point. If she does not have adequate protection (she is wet, her coat was shredded, she lost her gloves or boots, etc.), the Endurance Point loss rises to D6 over the same time period. A character reduced to five Endurance Points in this way suffers severe frostbite (the kind that requires amputation of toes or fingers). Characters reduced to zero Endurance Points die from exposure.

**Snowblind:** Staring out across the brilliant white plains is hard on the eyes. Every day spent in anything but forest requires a Constitution and Survival (Arctic) Task roll to avoid snowblindness. Those who fail the roll are effectively blind (they can see blurry shapes but no details). All skill Tasks in which sight is involved require two additional Success Levels (or more for fine work). Snowblindness fades after eight hours spent resting the eyes in dim or dark light.

**Mountain Climbing:** The Yukon is covered in steep mountains. The party must climb several of these in their mad flight from the zombies. Treacherous avalanches (see above), loose rocks, and zombies at the top and bottom of the climb should make the trek even more dangerous.

Remember too that the party likely has no climbing equipment. If they do not take precautions against falling, they are quite likely to plummet to the cold, spine-shattering ground below. Worse, the soft snow might mean a character with broken bones or paralysis could live—for a time. It is easy to imagine the horror of the rest of the group as a companion with two broken legs is swarmed by flesh-eating dead below.

## Conversions

*Deadlands* is a family of roleplaying games produced by Pinnacle Entertainment Group, founded by the author of this book, Shane Lacy Hensley. The primary setting for *Deadlands* is the "Weird West," circa 1877 (stand-alone, but fully compatible, *Deadlands* games have been set in the Wasted West and the Way Out West). Like *Fistful o' Zombies*, the *Deadlands*: *Weird West* game is about gunslingers and zombies, as well as a host of other horrors. The Weird West also has a heavy dose of steampunk, with flying machines, steam wagons, and airships.

Many fans of *Deadlands* are also fans of *All Flesh Must Be Eaten* and vice-versa, so the publishers at Eden and the head honchos at Pinnacle decided to produce this chapter to allow you, the consumer, to play either of these games with whichever system you prefer—the *Deadlands* game system or Eden's **Unisystem**.

The guidelines below should help both players and Zombie Masters (Marshals in *Deadlands* lingo) transfer characters, creatures, and spells, but some fudging will almost certainly be required, particularly in skills, Qualities, and Drawbacks.

## Attributes

To convert Traits and Aptitudes from *Deadlands* to **Unisystem** Attributes and skills respectively, add the number of dice to the die type and divide by three. A 4d12 score, for instance, adds up to 16 (4 + 12). Dividing that by three gives us 5.33. Use true rounding to get a final score of 5. A score of 4d6 translates to three (10 divided by 3 = 3.33).

To convert from the **Unisystem** to *Deadlands*, use the following table:

| Unisystem | Deadlands |
| --- | --- |
| 1 | 1d6 |
| 2 | 3d6 |
| 3 | 2d8 |
| 4 | 2d10 |
| 5 | 3d10 |
| 6 | 2d12 |
| 7 | 3d12 |
| 8 | 4d12 |

. . . and so on.

*Deadlands* uses ten Attributes (called Traits) instead of the six used by the **Unisystem**. The Attribute Correspondence Table (see p. 137) shows how the Attributes relate. When averaging *Deadlands* stats (such as for calculating Dexerity), average the number of dice and die type separately and use the values in the formula given above. For instance, a character with 3d6 in Knowledge and 4d8 in Smarts is being transferred to the **Unisystem**. The average in number of dice is 3.5 (3 + 4/2 = 3.5). The average in die type is seven (6 + 8/2 = 7). When using the formula given above (number of dice plus die type divided by three), the character winds up with an Intelligence of four (3.5 + 7/3 = 3.5, rounded up to 4).

To go the other way, both Knowledge and Smarts in *Deadlands* are derived from Intelligence. An Intelligence score of four in the **Unisystem**, for instance, gives the character 2d10 in both Knowledge and Smarts in *Deadlands*.

# Attribute Correspondence Table

| Unisystem | Deadlands |
|---|---|
| Strength | Strength |
| Dexterity | Average of Deftness and Nimbleness |
| Constitution | Vigor |
| Intelligence | Average of Knowledge and Smarts |
| Perception | Cognition |
| Willpower | Spirit |

Mien and Quickness are ignored when transferring characters between the two game systems.

## Secondary Attributes

Secondary Attributes in both games are derived from a character's base statistics and should be figured accordingly.

# Skills

## Unisystem to Deadlands

Use the *Deadlands* Skill Correspondence Chart (see pp. 138-139) below when transferring a character from the **Unisystem** into *Deadlands*. This translates skills into Aptitudes.

**Concentrations:** Some *Deadlands* skills have concentrations. For instance, a character with Shootin': pistols, rifles, and shotguns is equally good with all three types of weapons. If a **Unisystem** character has skill levels in Guns (Handgun), Guns (Rifle) and Guns (Shotgun), compute the *Deadlands* skill at whatever **Unisystem** skill is highest, then give him Concentrations in all other related skills. If the hero's Guns (Handgun) skill is highest, for example, use that to figure his *Deadlands* Shootin' skill, then give him Concentrations in pistols, rifles, and shotguns.

## Deadlands to Unisystem

Because many *Deadlands* skills are more open-ended (such as Academia, which covers any academic area of interest), some entries in the **Unisystem** Skill Correspondence Chart (see pp. 139-140) say "By Concentration." Academia: occult, for instance, translates into Occult Knowledge in *All Flesh Must Be Eaten*. Academia: ancient Roman civilizations becomes Humanities (Ancient Roman). Similarly, Arts: dancin' becomes Dancing in the **Unisystem**. If there is any confusion, the Zombie Master (Marshal) has the final say. In general, however, when skills do not correspond exactly, simply ask yourself what subject or area the skill covers. Odds are, both systems have some way of dealing with such a task.

If a skill has multiple Concentrations (such as Shootin'), the character gets the full skill with each type of weapon. A character with Shootin': pistols and rifles, for instance, gets his full value in Guns (Handgun) and Guns (Rifles).

# Deadlands Skill Correspondence Chart

| Unisystem | Deadlands | Unisystem | Deadlands |
|-----------|-----------|-----------|-----------|
| Acrobatics | None (*Deadlands* uses Nimbleness Trait) | Gambling | Gamblin' |
| Acting | Arts: acting | Guns (Type) | Shootin': type |
| Beautician | Professional: beautician | Haggling | Persuasion |
| Brawling | Fightin': brawlin' | Hand Weapon (Type) | Fightin': type |
| Bureaucracy | Professional: bureaucracy | Humanities (Type) | Professional: (type) humanities |
| Cheating | None (add +1 skill level to Gamblin' for every two levels in Unisystem Cheating, or a character may opt to translate this skill into the Bluff Aptitude) | Instruction | Professional: instruction |
| | | Intimidation | Overawe |
| | | Language | Language |
| | | Lock Picking (Type) | Lockpickin' |
| | | Martial Arts | Fightin': brawlin'* |
| | | Mechanic | Tinkerin' |
| Climbing | Climbin' | Medicine (Type) | Medicine: surgery |
| Computers | Science: computers | Myth and Legend (Type) | Academia: myth and legend |
| Computer Hacking | Science: computer hacking | | |
| Computer Programming | Science: computer programming | Notice | Search |
| | | Occult Knowledge | Academia: occult |
| Craft (Type) | Trade: type | Pick Pocket | Sleight o' Hand |
| Dancing (Type) | Arts: dancing | Piloting | Drivin': type |
| Demolitions | Demolition | Play Instrument | Arts: playin' |
| Disguise | Disguise | Questioning | Professional: questioning |
| Dodge | Dodge | Research/Investigation | Search |
| Driving (Type) | Drivin': type | Riding (Type) | Ridin' |
| Electronic Surveillance | Professional: electronic surveillance (although not appropriate for most Weird West settings) | Rituals (Type) | Rituals |
| | | Running (Type) | None |
| | | Sciences (Type) | Science: type |
| | | Seduction | Persuasion |
| Electronics | Science: electronics | Singing | Arts: singin' |
| Engineer (Type) | Science: (type) engineering | Sleight of Hand | Sleight o' Hand |
| | | Smooth Talking | Persuasion |
| Escapism | Nimbleness or Deftness Aptitude | Sport (Type) | Professional: (type) sport |
| Fine Arts (Type) | Arts: type | Stealth | Sneak |
| First Aid | Medicine: general | Storytelling | Tale Tellin' |

# Deadlands Skill Correspondence Chart (cont.)

| Unisystem | Deadlands |
|---|---|
| Streetwise | Streetwise |
| Surveillance | Professional: surveillance |
| Survival | Survival |
| Swimming | Swimmin' |
| Throwing | Throwin' |
| Tracking | Trackin' |
| Trance | None |

| Unisystem | Deadlands |
|---|---|
| Traps | Professional: traps |
| Uncon Medicine (Type) | Professional: (type) uncon medicine |
| Veterinary Medicine | Medicine: veterinarian |
| Weight Lifting | Professional: weight lifting |
| Writing (Type) | Arts: writing or Professional: writing |

*Martial arts have a supernatural tint to them in *Deadlands* and use very special rules. A character can either use that system or simply use Fightin': brawlin' instead.

# Unisystem Skill Correspondence Chart

| Deadlands | Unisystem |
|---|---|
| Academia | By Concentration |
| Animal Wranglin' | None |
| Area Knowledge | None |
| Artillery | Guns (Artillery) |
| Arts | By Concentration |
| Bluff | Smooth Talking |
| Bow | Hand Weapon (Bow) |
| Climbin' | Climbing |
| Demolition | Demolitions |
| Disguise | Disguise |
| Dodge | Dodge |
| Drivin' | Driving (Type) |
| Faith | None |
| Fightin' | Hand Weapon or Brawling |
| Filchin' | Sleight of Hand |
| Gamblin' | Gambling |
| Guts | None |
| Hexslingin' | None |

| Deadlands | Unisystem |
|---|---|
| Horse Ridin' | Riding (Type) |
| Language | Language |
| Leadership | None |
| Lockpickin' | Lock Picking |
| Mad Science | None |
| Medicine | General becomes First Aid, surgery becomes Medicine (Surgery), veterinary becomes Veterinary Medicine |
| Overawe | Intimidation |
| Performin' | Acting |
| Persuasion | Haggling or Smooth Talking (player's choice or split evenly) |
| Professional | By Concentration |
| Quick Draw | None (See the Fast as Hell Quality, on p. 29) |
| Ridicule | None |
| Ritual | Ritual |

# Unisystem Skill Correspondence Chart

| Deadlands | Unisystem | Deadlands | Unisystem |
|-----------|-----------|-----------|-----------|
| Science | Sciences (Type) | Survival | Survival |
| Scrutinize | Notice | Swimmin' | Swimming |
| Search | Notice | Tale Tellin' | Storytelling |
| Scroungin' | None | Teamster | None |
| Shootin' | Guns (Type) | Throwin' | Throwing |
| Sleight o' Hand | Sleight of Hand | Tinkerin' | Mechanic |
| Sneak | Stealth | Trackin' | Tracking |
| Speed-Load | None | Trade | By Concentration |
| Streetwise | Streetwise | | |

## Character Flaws

The list of Qualities, Drawbacks, Edges, and Hindrances is fairly large and complicated. To translate, simply look at the character's features and buy similar flaws or advantages from the other game. Some advantages translate very easily, some do not. If there is no equivalent ability, either redefine it if needed or ignore it as an advantage or flaw designed for that particular system. In the end, just make sure that the character is basically the same individual and that he has the appropriate number of flaws (no more than 10 points of Hindrances in *Deadlands* or Drawbacks in **Unisystem**).

## Deadlands Arcane Backgrounds

*Deadlands* has several unique character types, each with their own spells, skills, or abilities. Hucksters, for instance, are cardsharps who use secret spells encoded in Hoyle's Book of Games to sling incredible hexes. Mad Scientists can use the power of magical ghost rock to make amazing steampunk inventions. Neither of these translates directly into the **Unisystem**, and unfortunately, there is no space in this book to properly cover the over 500 spells, gizmos, and miracles available in the *Deadlands* game. Below is a quick method to use some of these abilities in the **Unisystem**, however. No doubt some tinkering will be needed to use these in *Fistful o' Zombies*.

These following rules assume basic familiarity with *Deadlands*.

Also, damage-causing spells and miracles are subjective and must be decided by the Zombie Master. Spells that affect Wind should cause the loss of Endurance Points, however.

Note also that hucksters, the blessed, and other special character types may buy additional spells, miracles and powers as play goes on. In *Deadlands*, these typically cost five Bounty Points each. In the **Unisystem**, they cost five character points each.

**Hucksters:** Each spell is cast off the hexslingin' skill. This skill level should be calculated as usual (see p. 136). When casting a spell, the huckster makes a hexslingin' Task as usual. Each additional Success Level in the **Unisystem** gives him one extra card to use when making his hand. A roll of 11, for instance, gives the character six cards. Resolve the hex's effect normally and translate any rules as closely as possible.

**The Blessed:** The Zombie Master has two choices when allowing the Blessed of the Weird West into his game. First, he can simply make the character be Inspired. In that case, give the hero one **Unisystem** Miracle for every miracle he has in *Deadlands*.

The second method is to use the spells as written. In that case, give the character a new skill called Faith. When attempting to use a *Deadlands* miracle, he must roll the Target Number listed in that game. Resolve the miracle's effects from there.

**Mad Scientists:** Mad scientists are able to create new gadgets and gizmos. This is based on the Tinkerin' skill in *Deadlands* and the Mechanic skill in **Unisystem**. To create a gizmo, the player should construct the blueprint and assemble the components as usual. Then he rolls his Mechanic skill and adds one card to his poker hand for every additional Success Level. When using weird science devices, the Malfunction rules apply normally.

**Shamans:** Indian shamans in *Deadlands* have as many miracles available to them as hucksters. The Zombie Master has two choices again: either allow the player to simply play a Medicine Man as described in the Dances with Zombies Deadworld (see p. 108) or translate the miracles from *Deadlands*. In the latter case, use the shaman's Ritual skill to gain Appeasement points as usual. Each Success Level translates to a raise in *Deadlands*, granting him more Appeasement points if the ritual allows it. Appeasement points may then be spent on the miracles presented in *Deadlands*.

**The Harrowed:** In *Deadlands*, the dead are not confined to the villains. Especially tough heroes can return from the grave as well. All Harrowed have the basic zombie abilities as written below:

**Attributes:** As in life

**Weak Spot:** Brain

**Getting Around:** Like the living

**Strength:** As in life

**Senses:** As in life

**Sustenance:** Harrowed do not need to eat, but they can heal their Constitution level in Life Points per day as long as they devour at least one pound of raw flesh (animal, human, carrion, or otherwise)

**Intelligence:** As in life

**Spreading the Love:** None

In addition, undead heroes may buy Harrowed powers. These function as they do in *Deadlands*, though some modifications will be required. For the Marshal/Zombie Master, Dominion and the manitou that powers the Harrowed work normally.

# Index

Archetypes 40-43, 62-63, 80-81, 96-97, 114-115
   Bad Girl 97
   Bandita 40
   Cowboy 41
   Drifter 96
   Gambler 42
   Grizzled Veteran 80
   Medicine Man 115
   Saloon Girl 43
   Sioux Brave 114
   Singing Cowboy 62
   Singing Cowgirl 63
   Tough Gal 81
Autry, Gene 11, 47
Billy the Kid 11, 13
Bowie, Sam 21
Brevet 28
Bronson, Charles 12
Buffalo Bill 11
Calamity, Jane 11
Character Creation 29-30, 48-51, 69-70, 86-87, 108-110
   Starting Funds 30
   Medicine Men 108
   Qualities and Drawbacks 29-30
   Restricted Skills 30
Conventions 14
Cooper, Gary 12
Crocket, Davy 21
Custer, General George 11, 23, 28, 101-103
de Santa Anna, General Antonio Lopez 21
Earp, Wyatt 11, 25, 27
Eastwood, Clint 12
Equipment 39
Evans, Dale 47
Fanning 30
Hanging 33
Hickok, Wild Bill 11
History 20-25
   Buffalo Soldiers 23
   Bureau of Indian Affairs 23
   Cattle 24-25

Cavalry 28-29
Civil War 21
Donner Party 21
Gold Rush 20-21
Indian Wars 22-23
Iron Horses 24
Mexican-American War 21
Sheepherders 25
Slavery 22
Houston, Sam 21
Holiday, Doc 11
Horses 32
James, Jesse 11
Lancaster, Burt 12
Lassoes 30-31
Law 26-27
Law Men 27
Lee, General Robert E. 22
Leone, Sergio 12
Lexicon 14
Medicine Men 108
Money 38
New Rules 30-35, 52-53
New West 20
Old West 19
Oakley, Annie 11
Qualities and Drawbacks 29-30
   Addiction 29
   Baladeer 48
   Delusions (Prejudice) 29
   Fast as Hell 29
   Law of the West 49
   Minority 29
   Number One with a Bullet 30
   Resources 29
   Sidekick 50
   Status 29
   True Grit 70
   Wonder Horse 51
Rogers, Roy 11
Rogers, Roy 47
Sitting Bull 101-103, 111
Scott, Randolph 11
Showdowns 33
Sioux 104-108

U.S. Marshal 27
van Peebles, Mario 22
Wayne, John 12
Weapons 36-38
   Bow and Arrow 36
   Derringer 36
   Dynamite 36
   Gatling Gun 36
   Kentucky Rifle 36
   LeMat Pistol 37
   Napoleon Cannon 37
   Nitroglycerine 37
   Rifled Musket 37
   SB Percussion Pistol 37
   SB Percussion Musket 37
   Sharps Big .50 Rifle 37
   Tomahawk 37
   Volcanic Pistol 38
   War Lance 38
Wild West 19-20
Zombies 32, 57, 72-74
   Anasazi 74
   Bloody Old Muddy 120
   Cold 133
   Comanche 127
   Dancing 103
   Horse 32
   Later Batches 89
   Mouth Bleeders 72-73
   Scratch Wilson and First Batch 89
   Singing Cowboy 57

## Tables and Charts

Close Combat Weapons Table 34
Crime and Punishment 27
Essence Recovery 110
Guns of the West 34
Ranged Weapons Table 34
U.S. Army Battle Groups 28
U.S Army Ranks 28
Weapons Availability Table 35
Yukon Supplies 132

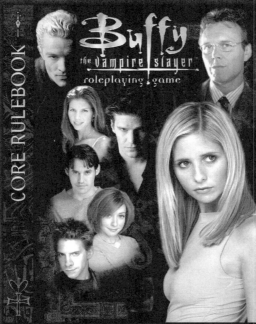

# ARE YOU READY TO RUMBLE!

## The rotten do-gooder face was still standing!

Despite all of the damage Marauder had done, all the rules he had broken, and all the underhanded tricks he had pulled, Crusher just stood there with that sickly lopsided grin on his face.

Marauder picked up a steel chair, spun, and confronted Crusher as his seemingly unstoppable foe slowly stalked toward him. Marauder took a step forward and with all of his might waffled Crusher square in the head with the chair. Crusher stumbled backwards and fell to one knee with a look of stunned amazement on his face.

No one could see it under his mask, but Marauder began to smile.

Step into the squared circle for the ultimate showdown!

*Zombie Smackdown* is a supplement for the *All Flesh Must Be Eaten* RPG. In it, you will find:

- Expanded rules for high-flying, bone-crunching wrestling action, including how to use Heat to pull off dramatic turns of events
- Zombie Cast Member creation for wrestling mayhem
- New Character Types and zombie Aspects to drop kick any face or heel
- Backgrounds on four different styles of wrestling and the weapons you can but aren't supposed to use in the ring
- Details on combining different wrestling styles
- Deadworlds featuring different wrestling styles and special Archetypes for each

EDN8005
ISBN: 1-891153-77-3
SRP: $23.00
Release: Summer 2003

**Go online and preorder at**
**www.allflesh.com**
or ask your local retailer to preorder a copy for you
**(or you will get busy with some**
**SMACKDOWN of our own!)**